"Parker's book is a serious w..s to and about black/white mixed-raced young women and girls living during perilous times. Situating her text in ethnography and critical race theory, Parker pens a message of hope during the rise of Trump offering the ethical principles of forgiveness, femaleship, fortitude, and freedom. Like a sentinel she calls out that liberation from racism will come when we receive people's plural identities as God's gift to the world."

—LINDA E. THOMAS, PhD, Professor of Theology and Anthropology, Lutheran School of Theology

"A masterful, empathetic storyteller, Evelyn L. Parker, as liberatory, compassionate bard, serves as pedagogical catalyst to move us to think about the complex lives and experiences of mixed-race girls, through the education of our imagination in *Between Sisters*. Communicating for understanding, she views forgiveness, femaleship, fortitude, and freedom as processes of emancipatory hope which can move us to solidarity for action. Like the parables of Jesus, Parker names the issues of privilege and systemic oppression, as a need to embrace hope and overcome the status quo. As gardener, Parker plants seeds of great intellectual curiosity; she fertilizes with lived experiences and invites us to partner with her in pulling out the weeds of cruelty, subjugation, and harassment amidst race, gender, class, and sexuality, dispelling myths of colorblindness and a post-racial, post-sexist, post-classist, gender-fluid world, embracing hope in dialog with the Holy Spirit. Using mixed media and her interdisciplinary gifts, she problematizes issues and seeks to dismantle oppression. She wants us to engage critical thinking, and own up to our complicity in the pains of the world. *Between Sisters* is a must-read for any interested in transformative pedagogy, adolescent girls, systemic oppression, and a theology and ethics of liberation."

—CHERYL A. KIRK-DUGGAN, Professor of Religion, Shaw University Divinity School

Between Sisters

Between Sisters

Emancipatory Hope out of Tragic Relationships

Evelyn L. Parker

FOREWORD BY Jack L. Seymour

CASCADE *Books* · Eugene, Oregon

BETWEEN SISTERS
Emancipatory Hope out of Tragic Relationships

Cascade Books
An Imprint of Wipf and Stock Publishers
199 W. 8th Ave., Suite 3
Eugene, OR 97401

www.wipfandstock.com

PAPERBACK ISBN: 978-1-62032-786-9
HARDCOVER ISBN: 978-1-4982-8757-9
EBOOK ISBN: 978-1-5326-3128-3

Cataloguing-in-Publication data:

Names: Parker, Evelyn L.

Title: Between sisters : emancipatory hope out of tragic relationships / Evelyn L. Parker.

Description: Eugene, OR: Cascade Books, 2017 | Includes bibliographical references and index.

Identifiers: ISBN 978-1-62032-786-9 (paperback) | ISBN 978-1-4982-8757-9 (hardcover) | ISBN 978-1-5326-3128-3 (ebook)

Subjects: LCSH: Racially mixed people—Race identity United States | African American women—Religious life | Womanist theology | Christian ethics—United States

Classification: BJ1275 .P25 2017 (print) | BJ1275 .P25 2017 (ebook)

Manufactured in the U.S.A.   APRIL 24, 2017

To Geraldine Parker, my mother, with love

Contents

Foreword

Among Sisters and Their Brothers

COMMUNICATION FOR UNDERSTANDING AND solidarity for action are important goals of education. So is inspiring hope for a better future. As a fine teacher, Dr. Evelyn Parker offers all of these in *Between Sisters*. The book is written explicitly for "black/white mixed-race young women . . . in a white dominant society where race is imposed on relationships and identity for the benefit of the dominant culture" (Introduction). Yet I believe that the book must be essential reading for a broader audience—particularly religious persons who seek to live faithfully in the everyday. *Between Sisters* invites conversation and inspires action "among sisters and their brothers"—indeed among all who care about mixed-race young women.

Communication for Understanding

In our current racially charged time, too much of both public and personal talk occurs without real conversation, by which I mean without adequately hearing the cries and challenges of those who are excluded and victimized. Rather than listening, "dominant-culture" persons (I am white and male) are often more concerned about the responses we will give or the defenses we will make. We are blind to the dynamics of the everyday realities that others face. We fail to understand that our experiences are different. We trust where others have learned to distrust. *Between Sisters* challenges our perceived notions.

By probing the interlocking dynamics of race, gender, class, and sexuality (that is, intersectionality) in our social fabric, Evelyn Parker elicits communication and provides opportunities for understanding. Sensitively yet insistently she demonstrates how race consciousness and race discrimination are embedded in the dynamics of our everyday living. Personal stories are her primary vehicles for communication. In each chapter, to illustrate the actual experiences of young women and offer pedagogical openings, she uses interview materials, historical examples, documentaries, novels, and films. To her primary audience, she offers language to name their own realities and strategies to address it. She opens the eyes of her secondary audience to see the realities and meanings to which we were earlier blind (or more accurately, that systematically we have been taught to ignore).

For all of us, her book is a superb example of the pedagogy that Paulo Freire called "problematizing."[1] She focuses our visions on the problems/realities in front of us. We cannot then ignore the voices, realities, and experiences of others. Sometimes we see them for the first time; other times we realize that we have been ignoring them for a long time. The consequence is that we either must address the problems or knowingly ignore them. For black/white mixed-race young women, the cause of despair and conflict is revealed as well as possibilities for hope and freedom. For well-intentioned religious educators and others who care for such young women, the claims of living in a post-racial world are revealed as false. For all of us, problematizing education causes us to engage social realities.

At the heart of the book and at the heart of her hope are Dr. Parker's deepest theological convictions and experiences of a God who offers unconditional love, of communion that unites, of

---

1. See Paulo Freire, *Education for Critical Consciousness,* reprint edition (New York: Bloomsbury Academic, 2013); and Myles Horton and Paulo Freire, *We Make the Road by Walking: Conversations on Education and Social Change* (Philadelphia: Temple University Press, 1990).

transformations that offer life, and of ways that human beings can work together for justice. These convictions are not simply theoretical "hopes" or "good words" for her. Rather they are good *news* that makes a difference and *grounded* hopes embodied in concrete actions. In fact, they extend Dr. Parker's profound concept of "emancipatory hope."[2] The processes of forgiveness, femaleship, fortitude, and freedom that frame the book shape the educational and spiritual process of emancipatory hope.

Each of these four elements invites persons to make decisions about how they will relate to others and what they will do. Confidently, emboldened by the "indwelling presence of the Holy Spirit," Dr. Parker proclaims "I have argued that hope . . . can truly liberate us from the interlocking and pervasive oppressions of racism, classicism, sexism, and heterosexism" (Chapter 5). Furthermore, she offers concrete clues in the conclusion, "Horizons of Hope for Mixed-Race Young Women and Girls," about religious practices that challenge the systems of domination. Without a doubt, she points to faithful education and action that address the black/ white mixed-race young women to whom she is writing.

Solidarity for Action

Through her excellent writing and teaching, Dr. Parker moves us to solidarity for action. She reminds us that all of us in the United States are embedded in the realities of race. Some of us take advantage of them every day. While I am the product of a working-class home and lived in a community defined as the "wrong side of the tracks" from which little of consequence was expected, I was still able to take advantage of being white and choosing options that were denied others because of their race or gender.

From the ravages of chattel slavery to calculated decisions promoting socioeconomic disenfranchisement, the US has deliberately limited opportunity for many on the basis of skin color. We often forget that current differentials in income and employment

2. Evelyn Parker, *Trouble Don't Last Always: Emancipatory Hope Among African American Adolescents* (Cleveland: Pilgrim, 2003).

are the direct result of political decisions about housing and education. One simple example is that after WWII, while white soldiers could use the GI Bill to borrow money for homes and to gain access to education, most of these benefits were denied to African Americans. Another that the implementation of the mid-1950s Supreme Court decision about the desegregation of schools was delayed significantly in many places and was not applied across many urban boundaries.[3] Such disadvantages add up.

Even more important, our social imaginations are shaped by race. "Race" is a social construction. Groups in power define the categories and, furthermore, who fits in them as well as the advantages or fears of each group.[4] We then learn racial categories as we simply move through our everyday realities. These categories fuel the ways we see others and expect them to act. They "control us!" Moreover, the meanings they engender are introjected into self-definitions. I know I can or cannot do something or be something because of how my imagination has been shaped.

Racism is thus maintained by housing, employment, and legal and police practices and by the *education of our imaginations*. Many of us with white privilege know these facts. We can even turn to educational studies that show the impact of the gaps caused by childhood access to reading materials or by the systematic dismantling of community supports for education. Nevertheless, too often, we simply "quote" these studies and their conclusions at the same time that we continue to live the ordinary moments of our everyday realities without making any differences. Our imaginations control what we do. They limit our choices.

---

3   See Michael J. Graetz and Linda Greenhouse, *The Burger Court and the Rise of the Judicial Right* (New York: Simon & Schuster, 2016).

4   See Leah Gunning Francis' provocative essay, "A Boy, A Wrestler and the Racialized Imagination." She describes how our social construction on race create a "racialized imagination" that controls how we see others and what we expect them to be and do. See wabashcenter.wabash.edu for a set of articles on race and teaching. Dr. Gunning Francis' essay is found at http://wabashcenter.typepad.com/antiracism_pedagogy/2014/12/a-boy-a-wrestler-and-the-racialized-imagination.html. See also Ta-Nehisi Coates, *Between the World and Me: Notes on the First 150 Years in America* (New York: Spiegel & Grau, 2015).

For example, Dr. Parker reminds us that black/white mixed-race young women despair as they say, *"That's just the way it is"* (Introduction). Their imaginations have been shaped to accept *"the way it is."* Similarly, the reality is that we who have been "privileged" also live as if *"that's just the way it is."* We know "in our heads" the causes and costs of racism. Yet, we deny them as we live our "privileges" (our head starts), assuming *"that's just the way it is."* Our imaginations shape what we see, inspire what we do, and direct both our advocacy and defensiveness. The myth that *"that's just the way it is"* must be challenged. Or as Dr. Parker illustrates, in her emancipatory education style, it is a problem to be posed and engaged.

To me, knowing and yet not acting in response is a form of blindness or, simply, sin. The emancipatory hope of the gospel is that the "the principalities and powers" (Romans 13), the systems of domination, are not the way living is to be defined. God calls us to work together for the realm of God—a realm that is real.[5]

Jesus' parables shocked hearers into addressing problems. In his emancipatory style, he problematized their everyday lives and shocked them into seeing something they were denying. For example, he challenged them to see what was really of value and that abundance was possible even in a time of despair (e.g. under Roman colonial control). Engaging problems offered options. New ways of interacting were promised.[6] As we know from the gospels, some heard, some denied, some walked away, some challenged; yet Jesus' emancipatory parables offered opportunities to live "abundantly" and not accepting that *"that's just the way it is."*

Conclusion

Honestly, through her attention to both communication for understanding and solidarity for action, Dr. Evelyn Parker offers

5 Jack Seymour, *Teaching the Way of Jesus: Educating Christians for Faithful Living* (Nashville: Abingdon, 2014): See Chapter 7..

6 See Amy-Jill Levine, *Short Stories by Jesus: The Enigmatic Parables of a Controversial Rabbi* (New York: HarperCollins, 2014)..

emancipatory hope. By telling the truth, by inviting us into the realities of others' experiences, as a parable-teller and educator, she "shocks" us all into seeing things we were denying. She calls us to solidarity and inspires actions that promote change. I will use Dr. Parker's book in my seminary classes. It offers the reader and/or the class a chance to understand others and to enlist us in mutual projects to confront "*the way it is.*" *Between Sisters* communicates a profound theological vision of hope—of how God calls us to share and work in communities with fortitude and faith. Thanks so much to Evelyn Parker.

Jack L. Seymour
Professor of Religious Education, Garrett-Evangelical Theological
Seminary

Acknowledgments

THE JOURNEY OF WRITING *Between Sisters* challenged me in many ways that have made me a better researcher and writer. Amid the many challenges, I was blessed to have folks who encouraged me to write this book. They felt it was an important practical theological project for those concerned about ministry to African-descended young women. This tangible community of grace asked me intriguing questions that honed my thoughts and ideas as well as giving me many smiles, hugs, and pats on my back to inspire me to complete this book.

The journey began during the Fall 2012 semester with students in my Southern Methodist University, Simmons School of Education and Human Development—Master of Liberal Studies class titled "Just Between Sisters." When I was asked to teach a course about race and women's experiences, I found opportunity and was granted freedom to structure the course around the book proposal that was being considered by Cascade Books. My fifteen female students of African, Asian, European, and Latina descent were the perfect conversation partners to hear and talk about my ideas and explore some of the novels used in this book. Some of my students were either biracial themselves or had biracial children. I am tremendously grateful to the students in the "Just Between Sisters" class.

I am equally grateful to students in my Spring 2014 and 2016 "Faith, Feminism and Public Policy" class at Perkins School of Theology, Southern Methodist University who heard and responded to snippets of my ideas from various chapters in the book during our class discussions. My students always ask questions that help me clarify my ideas.

Among the students in my "Faith, Feminism and Public Policy" class was Jessica Schell. Because of her brilliance, exceptional writing skills, and insatiable appetite for literature about feminist and womanist theory, I invited her to be my research assistant. She worked for me for three years until she graduated in May 2015. Jessica was the ultimate research assistant who asked me provocative questions and found amazing literature for me to read that advanced this project. Jessica's contributions are priceless and for which I am eternally grateful. Since Jessica's graduation, I have been without a research assistant. However, my administrative assistant has amazing abilities for editing and working with written texts. I wish to thank Brennan Blair for compiling the bibliography of this book.

I am indebted to my colleague and friend, Jack Seymour, who wrote a provocative foreword for this book beckoning a broader audience in light of the ongoing problem of race in the United States.

Words are insufficient to express my gratitude to Ulrike Guthrie, my personal editor. She is an editor par excellence. Uli worked patiently and tirelessly with me to polish this manuscript into the book that I hope you will enjoy. She is an editor who teaches and encourages you as she works with you to produce a good manuscript.

Last, but certainly not least, I owe a debt of gratitude to Cascade Books for their interest in and commitment to publishing this volume.

Introduction

Emancipatory Hope in a Racialized Society

Between Sisters proposes *emancipatory hope* as an effective response to racism and the simultaneous gender, class, and sexual oppression of African-descended women and girls in contemporary North American society. How can African-descended women, particularly black/white mixed-race women, hope in a society where race matters? How can black/white mixed-race young women experience a liberating hope in a white-dominant society where race is imposed on relationships and identity for the benefit of the dominant culture? How can a biracial young woman thrive in an allegedly but not actually post-racial society? I suggest that the hope that liberates women from the interlocking oppressions of racism, classism, sexism, and heterosexism comes through a process of *forgiveness, femaleship, fortitude,* and *freedom*. This process helps us prevail against a racialized society and imagine a post-racial society in the United States of America.

Though the United States of America is a society where abundant racial discrimination happens, some people believe we have entered a post-racial society. Neoliberals and ethnocentric nationalists argue that biracial and multiethnic "individuals and families will lead to the end of a race-conscious and racially-discriminatory society in the United States."[1] This book problematizes this form of mixed-race hegemony to say that societal problems of race are

1. Jolivette, ed., *Obama and the Biracial Factor,* 4.

1

embodied in the black/white mixed-race person and are revealed through their relationship with other racial/ethnic persons. *Between Sisters* focuses on relationships of black/white mixed-race young adult women that are flawed and dysfunctional due to interlocking oppressions of race, class, gender, and sexuality. I posit that the dysfunctional nature of relationships of the black/white mixed-race young woman is not entirely of her own making but is the result of the prevailing white dominant ideology that shapes the economic, political, and social policy that governs life in the United States.

The peculiar nature of relationships between black/white mixed-race young women and other women who are African- or European-descended is rooted in the historical stereotype of the tragic mulatta, an "unabashed creation of the White imagination"[2] about mixed-race, black and white, enslaved women and girls in antebellum literature. Some literary critics argue that the phrase "tragic mulatto" dates back to Sterling Brown's *The Negro in American Fiction* (1937) in which "a single drop of midnight in her veins" will cause the mixed-race figure to "go down to a tragic end."[3] Abolitionist writers of both races used the trope to investigate whether mixed-race enslaved persons and their children could achieve freedom and prosper in the larger mainstream culture.

The contemporary tragic mulatta stereotype is consistent with its historical roots. It is a derogatory trope found in literature, film, music, and folklore that describes a black/white mixed-race female who is intellectually, physically, sexually, emotionally, and spiritually inept and calamitous.[4] The tragic mulatta is the source and methodological framework for arguing that *emancipatory hope* arises out of complicated mixed-race women and girls' relationships. The problem of race/racism and stereotypes about

---

2. Townes, *Womanist Ethics and the Cultural Production of Evil*, 85.

3. Raimon, *The "Tragic Mulatta" Revisited*, 5.

4. Suzanne Bost's work, *Mulattas and Mestizas: Representing Mixed Identities in the Americas, 1850–2000*, is the primary influence on this definition of the tragic mulatta.

Colorc blind racism (handwritten)

biracial women such as the tragic mulatta suggest that the United States of America is far from being a post-racial nation.

The purported post-racial era is a sociohistorical period that ignores race and racial identity in pursuit of a color-blind society.[5] A post-racial society suggests that race/ethnicity and skin color do not matter in sociopolitical settings where policies that impact access to resources are determined. The landscape of post-racial ideologies is captured in three particular notions: that the popularity and immense success of figures such as Oprah Winfrey, Condoleezza Rice, and Colin Powell signifies that race no longer differentiates North Americans; in the increased support for the "extension of civil rights to previously disenfranchised racial groups"; and in the widespread optimism about racial dynamics.[6]

A post-racial society is colorblind, which means skin color as well as perceptions and stereotypes about the worth of racial/ethnic groups do not matter. While some argue that racism is strictly the result of the prejudice and overt actions of a few people who participate in the Ku Klux Klan or other contemporary militias in the North American context, this is far from the reality.[7] Such a restrictive notion ignores that "racism forms a social system in which we all participate" and the majority "of racial practices, events, behaviors, and cognitions in the public sphere have become normative, subtle, institutionalized, and apparently non-racial."[8] This colorblindness or "colorblind racism," argue Eduardo Bonilla-Silva and Victor Ray, is:

> anchored on the abstract use of the principles of liberalism to manufacture apparently non-racial explanations on all sorts of race-related matters. Hence, our main ideological enemy today talks in a color-blind fashion, tells us *I am not a racist, but* [...] looks like many of you in the audience, and may even support Obama! Accordingly, color-blind racism, whether expressed in angry

5. Wise, *Colorblind*, 24.

6. Sewell, "Moving Beyond Race," lines 7–10.

7. Bonilla-Silva and Ray, "It's Real!" 47.

8. Ibid., 48–49.

fashion (à la Geraldine Ferraro) or in a polished liberal, manner (as it is expressed in White academia), is the real ideological problem today and is the most significant political tool whites use to explain and ultimately, justify, the contemporary racial order of things.[9]

Colorblindness is racism veiled as abstract liberalism. It is a pretense for change in policies that would bring about racial equality and equal opportunities.[10] Colorblindness focuses on commonalities between African American, Asian, Latino/a, Native American, and multiethnic people. This ideology posits that treating individuals as equally as possible, without regard to race, culture, or ethnicity, is the best way to end discrimination.[11]

Though this book argues that North American society, specifically the United States of America, is *not* a colorblind or post-racial society, it does not say that a post-racial society is impossible. For to be Christian means to live in hope in spite of seemingly hopeless situations like racism. This book argues that hope liberates African-descended women and girls, particularly black/white mixed-race young women, from interlocking oppressions of racism, classism, sexism, and heterosexism and moves toward a colorblind society can come through a process of forgiveness, femaleship, fortitude, and freedom.

This book significantly foregrounds the proliferation of black/white mixed-race women and girls since the civil rights era of the fifties and sixties in the United States. This period witnessed the Supreme Court's repeal of states' miscegenation policies. Yet it was not until the year 2000 that Alabama removed its miscegenation law from state policies. The post-civil rights era also witnessed the disintegration of traditional constructs of race and the emergence of new ones advocated by a newly visible cadre of mixed-race persons who have claimed a place in US society.[12] In addition to this, the multiethnic movement pressured the US government

9. Ibid., 49.

10. Bonilla-Silva's term, "Abstract Liberalism," 9–19.

11. Williams, "Colorblind Ideology is a Form of Racism," 5–7.

12. Kilson, *Claiming Place,* 3.

to change the identifying ethnic categories in the 2000 census to allow individuals to select as many categories as they feel represent them.[13] True, these historical changes hold great meaning for all mixed-race persons, including black/white ones, but I would argue not to the extent some biracial persons believe, who think they are the "hope" for ending racism and racial discrimination in the United States. Instead, I argue that a hope that liberates us from racism is found in God's gift of difference, in relationships, and specifically in the morass of relationships where differences collide. *Between Sisters* focuses on women and girls who are of black/white mixed-race descent as a "case study" in order to bring to the fore interconnected dimensions of race, gender, class, and sexuality in the relationships of women and girls who are racially/ethnically different, with the goal of bringing to consciousness an emancipatory hope.

Although black/white mixed-race males, like President Obama, experience racial pressure, women and girls are particularly sensitive to intersecting issues of race and gender oppression,[14] and this vulnerability impacts racial identity development. Biracial girls' vulnerability is heightened by pressure to meet Eurocentric beauty standards in US society, to resist stereotypes, and to negotiate tensions between light-skinned and dark-skinned girls.[15]

The experiences of black/white mixed-race young women have implications for other African-descended women. *Between Sisters* is important for other African-descended women in two ways: first, it affirms God's creation of African-descended women and girls and that as God's creatures they have unique abilities to co-create and care for all of God's creation in a world that relegates African-descended women to the bottom of society. In her novel, *Their Eyes Were Watching God*, Zora Neale Hurston wrote that the black woman is the "mule uh de world" to illustrate the existential reality of black women in a white-dominated patriarchal society.[16]

13. Ibid., 5.

14. Rockquemore and Laszloffy, *Raising Biracial Children*, 131.

15. Ibid., 135.

16. Hurston, *Their Eyes Were Watching God*, 14.

Through Janie Stark's grandma's character, Hurston asserts that white men possess all human power and can only maintain economic, political, and social power by subjugating black men who in turn subjugate black women.[17] We recognize that black women are the mules of the world because their interests and well-being are not included in governmental policies or given social credibility in many African American communities. Yet while the burden of being black and female in a sexist and racist North America has been and continues to destroy some black women, it fortifies the resolve of other black women. From those that survive the curse of being the "mule uh de world," we can find examples of how black women live out *emancipatory hope*—hope that frees.

Second, the book showcases African-descended women's relationships as generative life-giving sites for God's liberating hope. A number of sources that include memoirs, formal and communal historical accounts, testimonials, and a cadre of black female writers attest to the power of black women and their ability to be relational, even with those who spitefully use and abuse them.

Among the many possibilities we could use to illustrate the relationships among black women are the women in Alice Walker's *The Color Purple*.[18] The characters of Celie and Shug in Walker's novel are drawn to each other out of mutual sexual attraction and because of Celie's need for affirmation of her womanhood, despite their mutual relationship with the same abusive man, Mister. Sexually and physically abused by her stepfather and by her husband, Mister, the pictures of Shug, a professional nightclub singer and Mister's lover, fascinate Celie. When Shug comes to town for a gig at a juke joint, she becomes ill and Mister brings her home to nurse her back to health. Initially Shug is rude to Celie even though she is captivated by Shug's manner and command of Mister. Eventually the women become friends and sexually intimate. Upon hearing that Mister beats Celie when Shug is away, Shug decides to move in with them. Yet Mister is unaware of the sexual intimacy between the two women. Eventually Shug helps Celie reconnect with her

17. Ibid.
18. Walker, *The Color Purple*.

6

beloved only sister, Nettie, who she presumed was dead, by helping her find letters from Nettie that Mister had intercepted and
hidden from her. Celie's rage at Mister for hiding the letters boils
over during a large family dinner, at which point Shug announces
that Celie will be moving to Memphis, Tennessee. While in Tennessee, Celie becomes a professional tailor and fashion designer.
Years later she returns to Georgia to claim the house and property inherited from her mother after her abusive stepfather passed
away. Celie establishes her clothing store and lives in her family
home. She discovers a reformed Mister with whom she reconciles
and becomes a friend. Through Shug and Celie's relationship,
Walker teaches us that Celie, an abused, castigated, and dehuman-
ized black woman can rise to a place of prominence and respect
financially, spiritually, emotionally, and socially. Through Celie's
experiences and relationships with God, and with Shug, Nettie,
and other women in *The Color Purple*, we discover how an abused
and beaten-down woman can rise in hope. Whether writing about
African-descended persons as black/white mixed-race or other
ethnic combinations that include the black African, *Between Sisters* offers a unique perspective within critical mixed-race studies.

The disastrous experiences of black/white mixed-race young
women and their relationships with other women regardless of
their race/ethnicity, class, and sexuality are case studies for arguing a process of emancipatory hope as forgiveness, fellowship/
femaleship, fortitude, and freedom. Contemporary memoirs,
movies, documentary films, and fiction where black/white mixed-
race young women are the central characters/protagonists are the
sources of my analysis. These sources are rife with the themes of
the chapters that follow: forgiveness, fellowship/femaleship, fortitude, and freedom.

This book also argues that race and racism must be analyzed
simultaneously with other intersecting forms of oppression relevant to the lives of African-descended women. Such intersectionality occurs when "socially constructed categories of oppression
and privilege, such as race, class, gender, and age, simultaneously
interact to create unique life experiences . . . ; race, class, and gender

7

are inseparable determinants of inequalities that interdependently 'form interlocking patterns.'"[19]

If systemic oppression can be analyzed through single categories of race, class, gender, and sexuality, which categories are most relevant to the sociocultural context of North America? While some pundits debate economic oppression for the poor and middle class, patriarchy and gender oppression against women and girls, and oppressive religious and secular policies against same-gender–loving women and men, many other pundits argue that racism and racial oppression are obsolete in the contemporary US. Experts who argue the demise of racism as a viable category offer a counterargument that citizens of the US have evolved into a colorblind society or post-racial era. This book counters that race is still a viable category for analysis because racism continues in both subtle and blatant forms.

The Nature of Hopelessness in North American Society

In his rap single, "Changes," Tupac Shakur punctuates accounts of despair of inner city people in the form of poverty, violence, murder, and hunger with a chorus sampled from the 1986 song by Bruce Hornsby and the Range, "The Way It Is." Tupac raps, "that's just the way it is." He sees no change happening when he gazes into the eyes of racist people or when he pleads for holistic change that brings peace to a war-torn world. Tupac concludes, "that's just the way it is." "Some things will never change" completes that statement in Hornsby's original song. Like these artists, many people, including religious leaders and communities of faith, desire changes in a society filled with injustice and oppression but accede: *That's just the way it is. Some things will never change.* They think: Why bother changing systems of domination that psychologically and spiritually beat people into a catatonic state? The common citizen striving to feed her family, clothe her children, keep a roof over

19. Murphy et al., *Incorporating Intersectionality*, 7.

their heads, and keep them safe from harm usually does not have energy left to fight the powers whose policies cause her to struggle to obtain those very basic human needs. At best, she is aware of systems of injustice that cause such struggles, but typically she chooses to focus on the necessities of life for herself and her family, not because she doesn't care but because she's too exhausted to do more than that. She joins the chorus of *that's just the way it is*, because her priorities require her to focus on the present. She postpones considering confronting power structures that created the injustices she and others face.

On the other hand, some who say *that's just the way it is*, truly believe that struggle for basic necessities is their lot in life, so why bother to question or protest? Some even rationalize that the struggle is ordained by God to gain their complete faith. They believe that struggle and suffering keep them faithful to God. They use phrases such as "God brought me to it so I must go through it," as a way of saying that God designed suffering to gain our complete love and devotion. This rationale absolves men and women of even the smallest effort to confront political, economic, and social injustice. Hopeless religious folk of this type content themselves with the impossibility of a just society. They live in a chronic state of pessimism that paralyzes their will to respond to injustice, and join the unending chorus of *that's just the way it is*.

Such chronic despair and hopelessness paralyzes the will to imagine a future with possibilities. Chronic despair leaves one unable to act in a hope-filled manner when faced with unjust structures and systems. Chronic despair about systemic injustices of racism, classism, sexism, and heterosexism cripple the body, mind, and spirit and perpetuate doubt, apathy, cynicism, and nihilism. Women and men plagued with chronic despair are unable to anticipate a future with hope for themselves and their communities.

Such chronic despair can be the precursor to acute despair and can lead to internalized self-destruction, such as suicide, or externalized destruction, such as deadly violent crimes. We see chronic despair in African American college women who have a present rather than a future outlook for their lives.[20] Scholars who raised questions about race and ethnicity with respect to suicidal tendencies among such African American and European American college girls described hopelessness as a cluster of negative "expectancies concerning oneself and one's future life."[21] The research intimated that hopelessness for African American college women was different from that of European American college women. It also found that African American co-eds do not "consider their future outlook on life as often as European American women" and thus do not report having positive expectations. Researchers such as J. M. Jones argue that African Americans frequently possess a present time perspective; that is, "given past and ongoing experiences with racism and oppression among them, they generally tend to focus their thinking on the present."[22] Similarly, African Americans across generations are compelled to adopt a present orientation given that the past is too painful and theirs is a limited future.[23] As suggested earlier, certain religious beliefs reinforce such passivity and chronic hopelessness.

What does chronic despair look like in the context of a purportedly post-racial US society? How can African-descended women and especially those of black/white mixed-race hope in a post-racial society? What is the nature of hope for change in the midst of systemic oppression and the beliefs that *"That's just the way it is. Some things will never change"*? Such hope is *emancipatory* in nature.

Emancipatory hope expects the dismantling of systems of domination that include racism, sexism, classism, and heterosexism. It acknowledges agency in God's vision of personal and communal transformation from systemic causes of despair. Hope of this nature understands despair to be the result of systemic oppression of people who are marginalized because of their race, ethnicity, economic status, sexual orientation, and/or other causes

20. Lamis and Lester, "Risk Factors for Suicidal Ideation," 7.
21. Ibid.
22. Ibid., 7–8.
23. Ibid., 8.

of injustice. They suffer oppression from the ideals and practices of economically, politically, and socially powerful men and women. The despair of marginalized people ranges along a continuum of hopeless activities and beliefs, from viewing the state of things as status quo, *that's just the way it is,* to lethal despair in the forms of suicide and homicide. At best, hopeless people mutter *that's just the way it is* in the face of the widening gap between the rich and the poor; *that's just the way it is* to racial inequality; *that's just the way it is* to white supremacist patriarchal heterosexist intent woven into the fabric of its public policies, social practices, and ideological identity in the United States of America. Is emancipatory hope relevant or even possible in a twenty-first-century USA that is purportedly colorblind and post-racial?

This introduction has laid out the bleak sociohistorical and sociocultural contours of discourse on the relationships of African-descended women and particularly black/white mixed-race women. It has also suggested that *emancipatory hope* can overcome this bleakness. This liberating hope consists of a process of forgiveness, fellowship/femaleship, fortitude, and freedom. What follow are chapters that explicate this process of emancipatory hope.

Drawing on the movie *Skin,* the first chapter focuses on forgiveness as the starting point towards emancipatory hope. Forgiveness is a freely engaged upon process through which individuals and communities "move away from the overwhelming power of an experience of hurt or an injustice."[24] The process of forgiveness holds persons accountable for hurtful and unjust actions, for wholeness of self and community requires forgiveness—but not forgetfulness. Such forgiveness is an essential aspect of emancipatory hope. The tragic breach of a mother-daughter relationship due to skin color and racism such as we find in the movie *Skin* requires the journey of forgiveness. The process begins with recognition of the virulent nature of cultural practices and policies related to a woman's worth "determined on an ascending scale based on an admixture of Caucasian blood."[25] *Skin,* based on Judith Stone's

24. Marshall, "Forgiving Churches," 189.
25. Cannon, *Katie's Canon,* 72.

memoir, is a story of tragedy and triumph. Sandra, the protagonist, is born to white Afrikaner parents but has dark skin and African features, a recessive gene from the family's ancestors. Sandra is a middle-class child who grows up victimized by South African apartheid laws, Afrikaner racism, and a sexist society. Her loving relationship with her parents devolves into betrayal and rejection when she begins a love affair with Petrus, a black man. A focus on Sandra's relationship with her mother and surrogate grandmother, her Gogo, reveals the process of forgiveness that yields a liberating hope. Through this example, the chapter examines how women and girls model divine forgiveness that leads to hope.

Chapter 2 focuses on fellowship/femaleship[26] which springs forth from forgiveness. Fellowship/femaleship brings a liberating hope when what were once destructive relationships evolve into communion with self, others, and God. Fellowship/femaleship describes the amiable and antagonistic relationships between the mulatta, her mother, her father, siblings, and non-familial females and males. The chapter focuses on female relationships of young mulattas like Sandra that embody deep connection and sharing amid the painful circumstances of racial prejudice, racism, and gender violence. It focuses on fellowship as communion with friends, as exemplified in the movie *Mixing Nia* and the novel *The Girl Who Fell from the Sky.* Nia Evans is the central protagonist in *Mixing Nia* who struggles to find her true identity. Her quest is set into motion when her boss at a prominent New York advertising firm asks her to write an ad campaign for malt liquor targeting black kids. Nia quits her job and attempts to write a novel that incorporates truths from her life experiences as the daughter of an African American woman and a white Jewish man. While this journey of self-discovery involves a number of Nia's interpersonal relationships, I focus on her relationship with her best friends. Nia's relationship with Renee, who is black, and Jen, who is white, reveals the real and raw nature of femaleship.

26. The term *femaleship* is the appropriate term to indicate wholesome relationships among women and girls. Fellowship/femaleship indicates the transition from the first term to the next in chapter 2.

The novel *The Girl Who Fell from the Sky* by Heidi W. Durrow is the story of Rachel, who is black/white mixed-race. After surviving her mother's partially successful effort to kill herself and her children, Rachel struggles with issues of racial identity, stereotypes, physical appearance, and sexuality. Her relationships with her grandmother and aunt are key but unstable. Nonetheless, such femaleship with girlfriends, grandmothers, and aunts can approximate communion with God and is a foretaste of emancipatory hope. Through her example, this chapter asks how communion among women who acknowledge and celebrate their differences reflects communion with God, and suggests it is when that communion reflects the beautiful attributes of divine communion as innocence, loyalty, and honesty.

Chapter 3 describes the role of fortitude in emancipatory hope. Fortitude is intellectual and emotional strength to persevere against all odds. Fortitude allows one to confront difficult situations with courage, patience, and perseverance, as we see in this chapter in the relationships of the mulatta and other women. The chapter begins with Diane Nash and Ruby Doris Smith, two young adult civil rights activists during the 1960s, who enfleshed fortitude for the cause of racial equality.

Fortitude is also illustrated in the novel *Caucasia* by Danzy Senna, the focus of the chapter. It is a coming-of-age story of race and identity about two black/white mixed-race sisters, one dark and one light-skinned. The sisters are separated when their white mother's and black father's marriage fails. Birdie endures the pain of separation from her dark-skinned sister, Cole, who leaves with her father and his black girlfriend to find a life free of racism. Birdie enters a life of passing as Caucasian/white as she searches ceaselessly for her sister. In Birdie, a teenager, we see fortitude that rejects white privilege obtained by passing as white and that resolves to reunite with a sister whom she loves. Can a liberating hope evolve without fortitude among women and girls, regardless of their race/ethnicity?

Chapter 4 identifies the place of freedom in emancipatory hope. Here, freedom means flourishing in the possible while negotiating the impossible. Freedom is the ontologically thriving spiritual self and community. What signs are there of true human flourishing in the mulatta and her relationships? By juxtaposing the documentary film *A Knockout* with the commercial film *Pariah*, I set up a dialogue on the nature of true freedom. The chapter examines individual freedom through the lives of same-gender–loving young women who are black/white mixed-race and African American using a biographical documentary about Michele Aboro and interview materials of Dee Rees, screenwriter and director of *Pariah*. Freedom for Michele and Dee means claiming an identity that is authentic. Can one be materially free yet beset by racism and sexism? For Michele Aboro and Dee Rees, freedom means coming into your own true self. The quest for true freedom in this chapter also considers communal freedom of faith communities, particularly those congregations that receive same-gender–loving young women.

Chapter 5, *Emancipatory Hope and the Holy Spirit*, proposes the link between emancipatory hope and the Holy Spirit. How does God act in a purportedly post-racial society to bring about emancipatory hope? Shall we hope in God who gives the gift of difference and relationships? This chapter reminds us that the Holy Spirit is God at work bringing hope, even while we wait for "the redemption of our bodies" (Rom 8:23b) that are black, brown, white, and mixed-race. The Holy Spirit works in all bodies, not just biracial ones, to bring about a liberating hope. The Holy Spirit stirs up the impossible to become the possible as she "helps us in our weakness; for we do not know how to pray as we ought, but that very Spirit intercedes with sighs too deep for words" (Romans 8:26). The Holy Spirit works as we forgive, share femaleship, exemplify fortitude, and live in freedom.

These perspectives on emancipatory hope I then place in actual conversation with Karen Baker-Fletcher, a womanist systematic theologian, who argues that the Holy Spirit gives courage in the face of hopeless situations. Baker-Fletcher's notion of courage is similar to emancipatory hope as fortitude. Her ideas about the Holy Trinity support emancipatory hope as developed in the previous chapters. This chapter engages Baker-Fletcher's *Dancing with God: The Trinity from a Womanist Perspective* while discussing the role of the Holy Spirit in emancipatory hope.

The book concludes with womanist practical theological reflections on the Christian church and its role in modeling the process toward emancipatory hope for African-descended women, especially black/white mixed-race young women and girls. The conclusion offers a pathway toward emancipatory hope through forgiveness, femaleship, fortitude, and freedom for congregations that choose to be courageous through the indwelling power of the Holy Spirit. How does the church embrace the challenge to be the lighthouse of liberating hope for a world darkened by systemically oppressive forces of race, class, gender, and homophobia? What does the church need to consider about its nature and ministry in the world so that black/white mixed-race women and girls may flourish?

Between Sisters examines the tragic relationships of black/white mixed-race young women to argue that hope that liberates women from interlocking oppressions of racism, classism, sexism, and heterosexism comes through a process of forgiveness, femaleship, fortitude, and freedom. The book does not claim that black/white mixed-race young women and other biracial and multiracial people are the solution to racial oppression and themselves usher in a post-racial society. Contrary to this widely held argument among neoliberals and some mixed-race people themselves, the United States is a racialized society that is far from being post-racial. Yet I suggest that a way forward can happen if we realistically confront problems of race and interlocking oppressions that benefit white dominant culture while practicing gifts of the Holy Spirit that include forgiveness, femaleship, fortitude, and freedom.

The Holy Spirit, God at work in the world, does not render us weak and impotent citizens of the world but courageous and powerful divine representatives of the reign of God in the world. This premise is the bottom line for congregations who embrace their vocation as baptized Christians, to represent God's reign when the evil of a racialized society seeks to overpower the people of God.

The life and ministry of Jesus Christ perfectly modeled the reign of God in a world where evil was brazenly demonstrated by men with economic and political power. Like Jesus, who fought evil that oppressed the people of God, baptized Christians—the church—must embrace this ethos of Jesus Christ. By doing so, Christian congregations will transform the racialized society of the United States into a post-racial society where person thrive regardless of their ethnic heritage. At that point we will read Galatians 3:27-29 with new eyes.

> As many of you as were baptized into Christ have clothed yourselves with Christ. There is no longer Jew or Greek, there is no long slave or free, there is no longer male and female; for all of you are one in Christ Jesus. And if you belong to Christ, then you are Abraham's offspring, heirs according to the promise.

1

Forgiveness

The path to emancipatory hope for black/white mixed-race young women as well as all African-descended women and girls begins with forgiving those who have hurt them. Forgiveness is a process freely engaged in by individuals and communities to "move away from the overwhelming power of an experience of hurt or an injustice."[1] Forgiveness requires that one holds persons accountable for hurtful and unjust actions that include abuse, disloyalty, betrayal, and unfaithfulness. Such betrayal occurs among friends, coworkers in religious and secular institutions, in marriage relationships, among siblings, and among parents and their children. Those most intimately connected are particularly hurt by betrayal, and most in need of forgiveness. Pastoral theologian Joretta Marshall describes forgiveness as yielding liberation from bondage that allows one to live into a new relationship. She writes:

> Forgiveness is a subversive and relational process summoned into action among persons, families, and communities when an injustice or hurt has been inflicted. It is a process that invites individuals and communities to move away from the overwhelming power of a hurt or pain while, at the same time, holding accountable those who have inflicted injustice or injury. Through this

1. Marshall, "Forgiving Churches," 189.

process individuals and communities are liberated from the bondage of oppressive anger and hurt, freeing their energies to work toward building, nurturing and sustaining relationships of justice and care.[2]

A disrupted relationship that causes "intentional or unintentional pain, injury, trauma or injustice" signals the need for forgiveness.[3] We are created to relate human-to-human and human-to-divine. Relationality makes us human. When a relationship, a core aspect of our humanity, is fractured the natural inclination is to find ways to gather together the pieces of the fractured self, and this process of reconstitution begins with forgiveness.

In his instructions on prayer, the writer of the Gospel of Matthew indicates the importance of this relationality and the reciprocal nature of forgiveness for humankind. When we pray we are to say, "Forgive us our debts, as we also have forgiven our debtors" (Matt 6:12). This instruction comes with clarifying conditions in verses 14 and 15: "For if you forgive others their trespasses, your heavenly Father will also forgive you; but if you do not forgive others, neither will your Father forgive your trespasses." The failure to forgive in the human-to-human relationship jeopardizes the human-to-divine relationship with God. A focus on relationality merits specific attention given its relevance for a discussion on relationships among African-descended women.

Among women of African descent, any discussion of relationships has to go beyond blood kin to include othermothering and fictive kin. Othermothering describes the action of a woman who cares for a child not biologically related to her. These two persons are fictive kin to one another, just as are any number of persons in relationship who survive by helping one another. Patricia Hill Collins's epistemological framework for African American women notes such an ethic of care as one of several ways of knowing among black women.[4] The ethic of care informs the historical and

2. Marshall, "Communal Dimensions of Forgiveness," 53.

3. Ibid., 51.

4. Collins, *Black Feminist Thought,* 281–84.

theoretical understanding of "othermothering" in the black community.[5] "The concept of othermothering grew out of a survival mechanism prevalent during slavery when children and biological parents were separated at auction, and 'fictive kin' would take on mothering responsibilities for the orphaned children."[6] Black teachers in historically black colleges and universities as well as in predominantly white institutions of higher education have noted their practice of othermothering black students.[7] These relationships are captured in familial terminology that usually endears the black teacher to her students. Monikers that include mom, Mama Hawk, and auntie all signal some level of othermothering between a black teacher and her college students.[8] The practices of othermothering in the context of a college or university are mutually beneficial when they provide connectedness, fulfillment, and interethnic support and advocacy. They become harmful when boundaries are breached, teacher-student roles are confused or violated, and caring for a multiplicity of students' needs leads to teacher exhaustion or "care-sickness."[9] As with any relationship, othermothering practices between black teachers and their black and black/white mixed-race female students can result in overwhelming hurt if the relationship is fractured. Likewise, the practices of othermothering or fictive kin relationships among any and all African-descended women can be a tinderbox for injustice that requires forgiveness.

While intimate betrayal is typically obvious to others, institutional betrayal of groups of people can be subtle, elusive—and covered up by the institution. The hurt caused by institutional betrayal often causes unidentified pain that is difficult to locate, difficult because the responsibility for the hurt is often shared among many persons and systems and cannot usually be attributed to a single person. Consider religious institutions that fail to create

Systems

5. Ibid.
6. Mawhinney, "Othermothering."
7. Ibid., 215.
8. Ibid., 220.
9. Ibid., 223.

policies that protect children and women from violence and abuse in their congregations, or that have such policies but fail to enforce them. Ordinarily, women, children, and men go to church and to its many ministries expecting a safe and spiritually uplifting environment. So after, for example, a pastor rapes a teenager in that church, she is particularly traumatized; she is betrayed not only by a trusted leader but by the institution that employs and endorses him, an institution that perhaps even allows the leader to continue in his role when his crime has been revealed. So while this chapter focuses on forgiveness of intimate betrayal between mixed-race young adult women and their mothers, as you read, keep in mind also this connection between intimate and institutional betrayal, particularly betrayal by the institutional church.

Countless memoirs, poems, novels, biographies, and movies describe the powerful pain one feels from being betrayed by a friend, lover, sibling, or parent. I describe only three here, and do so only briefly: Sonia Sanchez's *Wounded in the House of a Friend*, Toni Morrison's *The Bluest Eye* and *Beloved*, and Judith Stone's biography of Sandra Laing *When She Was White* and the movie *Skin* based on it. Poet and activist Sonia Sanchez describes the trauma of betrayal between a married couple in "Wounded in the House of a Friend." [10] Sanchez suggests that when a husband betrays his wife, the wife often seeks reconciliation. Yet despite many attempts to do so, the wounded wife in Sanchez's poem does not reconcile with her husband. Indeed, neither the husband nor the wife suggests their ultimate goal is forgiveness. Sanchez leaves the reader with the sense that betrayal in an intimate relationship can cause unspeakable pain that sometimes cannot be healed.

Toni Morrison captures the pain of betrayal that a vulnerable little girl feels when her father rapes her and her mother does not rescue her.[11] Such was the experience of Pecola in Morrison's novel, *The Bluest Eye*. Pecola's drunken father, Cholly, rapes her while she is washing dishes. Cholly's violent act of betrayal was so traumatic that Pecola passed out from the pain and shock. Morrison writes:

10. Sanchez, *Wounded in the House of a Friend*, 3–10.
11. Morrison, *The Bluest Eye*, 161–63.

"So when the child regained her consciousness, she was lying on the kitchen floor under a heavy quilt, trying to connect the pain between her legs with the face of her mother looming over her."[12] Earlier in the novel Morrison makes it clear that Pauline, Pecola's mother, does not love her children or her husband but the white family, the Fishers, for whom she works.[13] Pauline found beauty in the Fishers' home and their praise of her service. For her part, Pecola found beauty in the blue eyes of little white dolls and she wondered how it felt to be loved and longed for like that.[14] Desire for love and beauty is entangled in the morass of betrayal that Pecola experiences from her mother who also experiences ongoing pain from her fighting with Cholly. And Cholly also has a history of childhood pain, the result of being abandoned and abused. However, the book's primary focus is on the relationship between Pecola and Pauline, and illustrates a mother-daughter relationship in which the mother does not rescue the daughter from trauma. Morrison does not explicitly suggest Pauline's need to seek forgiveness from Pecola but the reader surely knows that such betrayal merits forgiveness. Morrison indicates that implicit in Pecola's "desire was racial self-loathing."[15] Longing for love and beauty is connected to the deeper systemic issues of internalized racism that members of the black community feel.

Yet, personal and communal wholeness requires forgiveness of those who traumatize friends, lovers, and family members. Forgiveness yields wholeness without compromising accountability for the hurtful wrong committed by a person or group of people. Accountability from all parties and just actions in the wake of forgiveness requires healthy remembering.

---

12. Ibid., 163.
13. Ibid., 127–28.
14. Ibid., 9–32.
15. Ibid., 210.

Pain of Betrayal Between Daughter and Mother

The biography of Sandra Laing titled *When She Was White: The True Story of a Family Divided by Race*, written by Judith Stone in 2007, and the film based on it titled *Skin* (2008), is a fitting point of departure to discuss the process of forgiveness between a mother and daughter. The back cover of the biography neatly summarizes the story:

> When Sandra Laing was born in 1955 to a pro-apartheid Afrikaner couple in South Africa's conservative heartland, she was officially registered as a white child. But her brown skin and frizzy hair—resulting, her parents insisted, from an interracial union far back in her family history—caused the white community in which she lived to ostracize and shun her. When Sandra was forcibly removed from school and reclassified as "coloured"—of mixed race—the Laings fought their daughter's reclassification all the way to the Supreme Court. Their grueling battle proved futile when Sandra eloped with a black man, estranging her from her parents.[16]

Sandra's story, particularly that of her childhood and young adult years, fits the genre of the modern-day tragic mulatta. We have seen that the tragic mulatta motif implies that nothing good ever comes from the life of the black/white mixed-race woman. Sandra's skin color and other physical features that became much more evident during grade school made her a victim of the mid-twentieth-century South African apartheid laws—a complex set of social and economic policies instituted by the ruling political party that promoted white supremacy and enforced segregation. Unusually, race, gender, and class all intersect in Sandra's tragic mulatta story because of the context of apartheid in South Africa. The movie version of Sandra Laing's life story, *Skin*, follows the biography very closely except for the events and relationships that lead to the birth of four more children in addition to the two shown in the movie and events leading up to the death of her father. The

---

16. Stone, *When She Was White*, from back cover.

biography was actually commissioned to facilitate the writing of a screenplay for *Skin*. In the movie version of Sandra Laing's life, viewers are led to believe that her parents, Abraham and Sannie Laing, are initially unaware of their genetic heritage. The film offers tacit clues that Abraham has doubts about his wife's faithfulness regarding Sandra's conception. The series of events in the film lead to a fractured relationship between Sandra and her parents.

The film begins with the adult Sandra Laing traveling on public transportation to the polls to vote in South Africa's first democratic election in 1994, accompanied by her adult children, Henry and Elsie. A scene follows in which Sandra works in a factory and is summoned by her supervisor to give an interview to a television reporter. A colleague then approaches her for an autograph on the newspaper article whose headline reads, "Too Late for Sandra Laing." A large picture follows the headline, of Sandra and Sannie. Her mother smiles with her arm around Sandra. Clearly unsettled by the picture, she refuses to give the autograph and hurriedly pulls away in a fury of flashbacks of her mother, father, and brothers, Leon and Adriaan, some years earlier. We see a happy ten-year-old Sandra dressing for travel to a boarding school that she and her brother Leon, the eldest Laing child, will attend. During the drive her doting parents show their love with hugs, kisses, and little songs composed just for Sandra. The scene depicts a happy time when Sandra Laing will live out her parents' Afrikaner middle-class life of being able to send their children off to boarding school. However, Sandra's boarding school days are short-lived; school officials dehumanize her through unexplained corporal punishment and verbal attacks. Her classmates are more transparent with their mocking and sneering at Sandra's skin color, kinky hair, and round hips. The shaming and ostracizing events climax when the headmaster brings in a doctor to measure Sandra's physical features and she asks, "Am I sick?" The headmaster obtains legal documents to reclassify Sandra as colored and removes her from the boarding school. The headmaster and two police officers drive her back to her parents, Abraham and Sannie. Though her parents are outraged with the decision of the school authorities, they leave her brother, Leon, at the boarding school.

Then and always, Sandra's mother Sannie is compassionate and loving in the midst of her husband's constant questions about her faithfulness in the conception of their daughter. Sannie's response signals that the doubting Abraham has long questioned Sandra's difference, imputing it to Sannie's infidelity. Sannie appears to be Sandra's champion. Unlike Abraham, she advocates for Sandra's dignity and worth, even though both parents fight the legal authorities about the classification of her racial identity.

Throughout her preteen years, Sandra goes before authorities who examine her hair and body parts to determine her racial classification. Sannie and Abraham continue to express their love for her and their determination to change her classification back to white Afrikaner. Her mother never fails to affirm Sandra as her daughter. Yet her father rubs skin lightening lotion on Sandra's face that he blows on to soothe the burning effect. Sandra overhears her brother Leon express his concern that the child his pregnant mother Sannie is carrying will turn out to be dark skinned like Sandra. In desperation, Sandra tries to rectify the family's shame by mixing and applying chemicals to brighten her skin, which results in severe skin and lung burns and coughing caused by the fumes. Sannie rescues Sandra from this painful "whiting ordeal" by washing the chemicals off her skin and applying calamine lotion. Abraham continues his appeals to change her racial identification all the way to the South African Supreme Court, where a geneticist testifies that all Afrikaners have a Bantu gene in their bloodline and that on occasion a child is born phenotypically showing the "throwback gene" or polygenetic inheritance. Subsequently the Supreme Court makes a decision denying the Laings' appeal to change Sandra's racial classification back to white. Soon after, Adriaan is born. Although the little baby boy is dark skinned like Sandra because he too manifests polygenic inheritance, at first Sannie remarks that he looks just like his father, Abraham.

Time passes, and the South African government decrees another racial-identity policy that indicates that descent rather than skin color determines racial identity. Upon hearing this, her father rushes to tell the family the good news that Sandra has been reclassified as white. She is placed in a girls' boarding school.

The next scene opens with Mrs. Sannie Laing picking up eighteen-year-old Sandra from school for a holiday. She returns home happy to see her little curly haired, light brown-skinned brother, Adriaan, who adores her and wants to play. She asks him to wait until she speaks with their father. As she stands behind the door of the family's general store, a young black African man is taken by her coyness and beauty. Sandra is embarrassed by the eye-to-eye contact. Her father, seeing the two gaze at each other, comments that a general store is no place for a young lady. He shows her a typewriter that he hopes will help her learn the skill of typing for obtaining a future job.

While Sannie encourages her to date white Afrikaner young men by buying her new dresses and teaching her how to apply makeup, Sandra is uninterested in the boys her parents select. On her first date with one of these white men, she slips out the window of the women's toilet to escape. Petrus, the young black man who saw her at their general store, sees Sandra hanging from the window, rescues her, and takes her home. Thus develops their affection for each other, an affection not sanctioned by her father. Sandra's choices for love and intimacy with a black man come to a head when her father realizes she is determined to be with Petrus. Her decision to leave with him drives her father into a rage; he burns all her personal items and declares her to be dead. Sandra's mother appears complicit in her father's behavior, choosing not to defy his decision to excommunicate Sandra. She is devastated by her mother's resolve to comply with her father. Her mother, who for years had supported and advocated for her, as she was first classified as colored and then reclassified as white, now betrays Sandra. When, after having her first child, Sandra reaches out to her mother, her father foils the plan to meet secretly. Sandra is unaware that her mother has attempted to meet with her, only to be thwarted by her husband.

The only way Sandra can assuage the pain of being betrayed by her mother is with a substitute mother, a "Gogo" or grandmother in Zulu, who serves as an othermother for Sandra. In time, the Gogo also serves as Sandra's midwife, advisor, and her advocate when Petrus becomes violent.

Sandra Laing's biography reveals more details about her relationship with Sannie, her mother, and Jenny, her Gogo during the time of estrangement between Sandra and her family. In *When She Was White*, her biographer, Judith Stone, describes Sandra's close relationship with Sannie from early childhood until Sandra went to boarding school in Piet Retief at the age of six. Sandra, the second child and only daughter, helped Sannie in the family's general store each day and they played games together.[17] Sannie taught her daughter how to plant, tend, and harvest vegetables.[18] When Sandra was sent home from boarding school at age ten for being black, she worked in the shop with her mother each day. She also studied math and social studies using books her father had purchased to teach her until he could get her back into school. Sannie would usually express her dismay when Sandra was derided because of her skin color. On one occasion Oupa Roux, Sannie's father, came for a visit and called Sandra a *Kaffir* or nigger girl for teasing him by hiding his pipe in the cushions of the sofa. While *Kaffir* was purportedly an affectionate nickname, Sandra, at the age of eleven, felt the sting in her grandfather's voice and ran to tell her mother. Sannie, furious, approached her father about the incident.[19] The bond between Sannie and Sandra grew even closer when she was homeschooled for three years. During that time Sannie became pregnant and had Adriaan. Sandra anticipated the birth of the baby and helped her mother care for him after he was born.

While Sannie defended Sandra from the racist language of her Oupa Roux, she was more restrained about objecting to Abraham's decisions about their daughter's race problems that included using the media to advance his campaign to get Sandra reclassified as

17. Stone, *When She Was White*, 30.

18. Ibid., 33.

19. Ibid., 103.

26

white. Sannie and Abraham would argue in their bedroom about decisions Abraham made, but Sannie rarely if ever spoke against him in public. Judith Stone indicates that Sannie was afraid that Abraham would kill her, Sandra, and himself because of honor and shame mores in white Afrikaner culture. Sannie also contemplated killing Sandra and herself because of the racist pressure of having a dark-skinned child.[20]

When Sandra was thirteen years old, she enrolled at St. Dominic's Academy in Newcastle, Natal province, the only school that would take a dark-skinned white child.[21] White was her reclassification after the 1967 decision by the Minister of Home Affairs. Upon coming home for a holiday, Sandra met Petrus, who was ten years older than her and married with three children. Her girlish infatuation grew into love for Petrus and they spent more and more time together whenever she was home. Sandra indicated that her mother knew of her relationship with Petrus, never tried to discourage her, and kept Sandra's involvement with Petrus from Abraham. Judith Stone, the biographer, clearly questions Sandra's memory and assessment of her mother, first, because both Mr. and Mrs. Laing were committed supporters of the apartheid regime; second, because psychologists who consulted with Stone detailed several coping mechanisms that included denial that would allow Sandra to cope with her abysmal reality at home and at school,[22] including that Sannie might not have sanctioned or accommodated Sandra's love affair with Petrus and yet could have worked to keep details of the affair from her husband. When Sandra eventually left home to live with Petrus and his family, Abraham vowed to kill Petrus and Sandra because of the shame she had brought him.[23]

Nora, the Laing's black housekeeper, also knew about Sandra's affair with Petrus. Nora was an "othermother" for Sandra during stressful times in the Laing household. Reflecting on Nora's presence in the Laing family, Sandra recalled: "Nora was like a mother

20. Ibid., 104.
21. Ibid., 117.
22. Ibid., 122.
23. Ibid., 141–42.

to me, and I loved her. When I was little, Nora put me on her back with a blanket while she worked."[24] Stone indicates that Sannie also confided in Nora, which was not an uncommon "relationship between employer and domestic helper . . . but it rested on a hideously unequal distribution of power."[25]

Jenny, Petrus's mother, was an "othermother" to Sandra when she went to live with Jenny and Amon Zwane in the black township of Dorsbult.[26] Jenny taught Sandra the duties of a Swazi wife that included sewing, cooking, and cleaning.[27] Jenny also taught Sandra the importance of mutual respect between a husband and wife, and other Swazi social customs.[28] Jenny treated fourteen-year-old Sandra as if she were her own daughter.

When Sandra left home with Petrus, she called her mother once a month.[29] At age sixteen, she became pregnant by Petrus with her first child. She recalled that while in labor she cried out for her mother, but that it was Jenny, Petrus's mother, who consoled her and helped with the delivery.[30] As soon as she was able, Sandra phoned her mother about Henry's birth and Sannie pleaded with Sandra to see her first grandchild. They planned the visit for midday so Abraham would not know about it, as he was unlikely to come home during that time. Stone records Sandra's recollections of the reunion of Sannie and Sandra:

> Mother and daughter hugged and cried . . . Sannie held Henry and kissed him. "She said, 'He's a beautiful boy.' We stood outside on the *stoep* for the whole visit. Sannie didn't invite Sandra into the house. She asked if Sandra was all right, and said she missed her. Sandra told her mother she missed her, too. "She said my father mustn't find me because he's very angry. The visit was only ten

24. Ibid., 121.
25. Ibid.
26. Ibid., 147.
27. Ibid., 149.
28. Ibid., 150.
29. Ibid., 151.
30. Ibid., 158.

minutes. My mum was scared my father would come. I just felt I had to show her my child. He was her grandchild. She was happy to see the baby. She wasn't angry with me and she didn't scold me. She was never really angry with me."[31]

On July 21, 1973, fifteen months later, Sandra had her second child, a girl that she named Elise. As before, Sandra called her mother with the news of her second child. Once again Sandra took her baby to meet her "white Ouma Sannie."[32] As before, mother and daughter hugged and cried and then Sannie sent Sandra home with food and clothes for her children. As Sandra was leaving, her mother told her that she and Abraham were thinking about selling their shops and moving elsewhere, but that she didn't yet know when their shops would sell or where they would move.[33] As during their phone calls and brief visits, Sannie encouraged Sandra to take care of herself. Then Sannie asked that Sandra "not make contact with her again,"[34] which Sandra recognized as being her father's and not her mother's idea. Thus began the long period of estrangement between mother and daughter.

However, Judith Stone questions Sandra's accounts of the mother-daughter relationship, noting Sannie's complicity with apartheid policies against racial mixing in any form. Stone, in consultation with psychologists and psychotherapists, argues that the trauma of Sannie's rejection of Sandra was so powerful that Sandra fabricated the congenial reunions with her mother. Also, when South African newspapers reported that Sandra was living with a black man and had children with him after the public struggle to get her reclassified as white, Abraham and Sannie felt they had to protect Leon, Adriaan, and themselves. Thus, they sold their property and moved away. Sandra wrote to her mother several times after the family moved away but never received a reply.[35]

31. Ibid., 159.
32. Ibid., 161.
33. Ibid.
34. Ibid.
35. Ibid., 163–66.

Sixteen years passed after Sannie told Sandra not to contact her again.[36] When Abraham, her father, passed away in 1988, Sandra lamented that she had never had an opportunity to ask for his forgiveness. Ironically, she was not concerned that her father never asked her to forgive him. Sandra took ownership of the Laing family's problems that she thought were due to her Bantu physiognomy, her living with a black man, and her having children with him.

Even though Leon and Adriaan worked hard to keep Sandra away from Sannie, two reporters help her reunite with her mother. During the reunion Sandra didn't verbalize words asking her mother for forgiveness, but she indicated that she just knew all was forgiven during their time of reunion.[37] "That Sannie might be the one requiring forgiveness was not a thought that occurred to Sandra at the time."[38] On a subsequent visit with Sannie, Sandra brought all her children to see their grandmother. Sannie died not long after the visits and phone calls from Sandra. "Though Sandra grieved for Sannie, the relief of feeling forgiven had already begun to lift the weight that flattened her heart for years, and to release complex emotions, long suppressed."[39] Sandra visited her father's grave some time before her mother's death and asked his forgiveness. In the closing chapters of her biography we discover that she also sought forgiveness from her brothers through letters and phone calls, yet only Leon chats with her—a small step toward forgiving Sandra at the close of the biography.[40]

36. Ibid., 200.
37. Ibid., 231.
38. Ibid., 230.
39. Ibid., 237.
40. Ibid., 249.

The Process of Forgiveness and the Fault of the Wounded

We learn from the movie *Skin* as well as from the biography *When She Was White* that Sandra desires deeply to reunite with her mother. It is in the biography that we discover her earnest desire to be forgiven by her mother, father, and brothers. That her family does not reciprocate this forgiveness is inconsequential for Sandra. What is important to her is that she engage the process of forgiveness by seeking the forgiveness of her parents and siblings.

The process of seeking and attaining forgiveness in the context of relationships can be likened unto a winding road on which one takes an unknown time to reach one's destination.[41] The dynamics may include:

> recognizing that a wrong has been committed, naming the hurt and pain experienced by the participants in a situation, allowing anger to be expressed by various parties, confessing one's own participation in hurting another, changing behavior so as to lower the chances of the same pain being inflicted again, and moving toward a reconciling stance with another.[42]

The process does not alleviate consequences of one's actions but it can change the relationship between participants.[43] Catherine T. Coyle discusses similar processes regarding interpersonal forgiveness that expand Joretta Marshall's processes quoted above into four phases—of uncovering, decision, work, and outcome or deepening.[44] Coyle is careful to point out that forgiveness and reconciliation are not the same. "Forgiveness is an internal response of one individual to another while reconciliation implies that two people, both the injured and the offender, choose to engage in some sort of relationship."[45]

41. Marshall, "Forgiving Churches," 190.
42. Ibid.
43. Ibid.
44. Coyle, "Forgiveness, Reconciliation, and Healing," 98–103.
45. Ibid., 97.

In Sandra's situation we can conclude that she decided to seek forgiveness of her parents and brothers as a means of survival and moving ahead in life. Ideally, she would also benefit from the help of a psychotherapist to heal from the atrocities of racism, sexism, and classism that were foundational for the severing of her relationship with her parents and brothers. The trauma of apartheid in South Africa that caused Sandra to live in denial of her parents' reasons for not accepting her skin color and her relationship with a black man as well as her obliviousness to political and social injustices suggests that all she could manage was to cope with her reality rather than move toward forgiveness. Sandra needed psychotherapy because of the trauma of apartheid. Psychotherapy could have helped her to negotiate the processes of forgiveness in a wholesome manner. Appropriate psychotherapy is essential for any black/white mixed-race woman seeking to be whole in a racist, sexist, and classist society. The work of skilled psychotherapists and their use of psychological models of forgiveness that intentionally consider the intersection of race, class, and gender issues is invaluable. At the same time other important aspects of forgiveness should accompany the psychotherapeutic processes of forgiveness.

Forgiveness amid Race, Class, and Gender Oppression

The meaning of divine forgiveness is exemplified in the life and ministry of Jesus Christ. His prayers, teaching, and healing in the New Testament Gospels reflect the practice of forgiveness. He took authority to forgive the sins of women (Luke 7:47–48) and men (Matthew 9:5) when faith of the individual or their friends was demonstrated. One could speculate about his multiple encounters with Peter on the meaning (Matt 18:21–22) and practice (Matt 25:69–75) of forgiveness. Peter's human nature demonstrates concern and failure about forgiveness. In contrast, the divine Jesus teaches and models forgiveness.

Theologians have defined forgiveness in a christological manner and have proposed relevant practices of forgiveness. Yet, as Jane McAvoy has noted, feminists and others have critiqued those theologians who argue for forgiveness as being a way of imitating Christ in "bearing the cost of forgiveness in one's body and soul" or the willingness "to embrace one's enemy in self-giving love."[46] These arguments are unhelpful for victims of abuse. McAvoy argues that examples from novels, specifically Sue Miller's novel *The World Below*, offers more concrete ways to imagine how to forgive.[47] For example, McAvoy points to the complexity of the relationship and power differential between the husband and wife protagonists in that novel as providing insight on the convoluted nature of forgiveness between married partners.[48] Judith Stone in *When She Was White* similarly points out the complexity of relationships between a daughter and her parents and siblings, a young woman and her common-law husbands and the other women in their lives. Stone's biography adds the dimensions of racism, sexism, and classism as they intersect in the life of Sandra Laing. In the biography, after Sandra has reunited with her mother, Sannie, we discover that class differences between Sandra and her family become a prominent factor in their relationship. Sandra, who is very poor, is given a portion of the money her mother received from the sale of their property. After Sandra's brother Leon discovers she is in contact with their mother, he offers her monthly payments to stay away from their mother. Because Sandra needs money to take care of her children, she takes the money but still continues to visit her mother. The prominence of money exchanges continues until the end of the biography. Thus, in the complex relationship of Sandra and her mother and brothers, we must note the added dimensions of race and class and Sandra's constant need to seek her family's forgiveness. In the instance of Sandra Laing's life, forgiveness in theory and practice can be imagined out of fractured relationships of black/white mixed-race women and their mothers when the one who has been hurt seeks forgiveness first.

46. McAvoy, "The Practice of Forgiveness in Sue Miller's Novel," 135–45.
47. Ibid.
48. Ibid., 141–42.

Yet a return to Christology for ideas about practices of forgiveness does hold potential. McAvoy's essay summarizes Gregory Jones and Miroslav Volf's comments respectively on Jesus taking on the cost of forgiveness through his death on the cross and Jesus modeling how to embrace one's enemy in love. I would suggest that Jesus, as completely human and divine, knew the importance of forgiveness for keeping human beings in relationship with each other when their relationships are broken apart. When Peter asked Jesus how many times we should forgive a brother or sister, intimating that seven times was the appropriate response, Jesus replies that in fact we should forgive seventy-seven times (Matt 18:21–22). His response to Peter suggests that forgiveness to restore a relationship is unquantifiable. The cost of maintaining human relationships includes the hard and ongoing process of forgiveness.

Jesus modeled the essentialness of human relationships. He sought to be in relationship with women and men across borders of ethnic, social, and religious difference. Clearly aware of traditions and mores of engaging women, Jesus breached traditions and customs to be in relationship with the Samaritan woman, those suffering from leprosy, and many other outsiders. The people Jesus chose as intimate friends—his twelve disciples, and the women who accompanied him—like him primarily were not from among the social elite. Jesus valued his relationships with people on the margins of society as well as those in the center and modeled the importance of maintaining his relationships with women and men. Thus, it is reasonable to believe that the practice of forgiveness was essential to maintaining his relationships.

God's gift of human relationality and the human will to nurture that gift is what makes relationships divine. Humankind was created to be in relationship with one another and therefore in relationship with God. The natural gift of human relationality with respect to black/white mixed-race women is affected by social and cultural practices of racism that taint the natural proclivity to embrace each other beyond differences defined by society and culture. Yet we can overcome such differences, not least through forgiveness. The starting point for forgiveness is examining what (in this case) women hold in common and acknowledging what sets us apart. Gender—our femaleness—binds women together. Regardless of whether a woman is rich or poor, white or black, her gender is the common denominator. So is our status as children of God. With the acknowledgment of such deep commonalities, forgiveness can move women forward out of the despair of injury from betrayal into grace-filled hope of healing.

2

Fellowship/Femaleship

FELLOWSHIP AMONG WOMEN AND girls, particularly between black/white mixed-race women and with other women, brings about emancipatory hope. Fellowship springs from forgiveness; without forgiveness there can be no true fellowship. Fellowship brings a liberating hope when strained relationships evolve into communion with self, others, and God. Fellowship captures the reality of amiable and antagonistic relationships between the mulatta, her mother, her father, siblings, and non-familial females and males. This chapter focuses on female relationships of the young mulatta that embody deep connection and sharing amid the painful circumstances of racial prejudice, racism, and gender violence.

Fellowship is a somewhat odd choice of word to describe women's relationships with other women. The word *fellow* has been used familiarly since the mid-fifteenth century to signify a man or male person.[1] However, the term fellowship also captures the nature of women's relationships as a deep level of companionship, intimacy, and friendship.[2] Another way to capture women's relationships with one another and with God is to create a word, and thus I suggest the gender-specific word "femaleship." Occasionally,

---

1. "Fellow," http://dictionary.reference.com/brouse/fellow.
2. "Fellowship," http://dictionary.reference.com/browse/fellowship.

I use the term *femaleship* as a synonym for fellowship to represent the deep relationships among women and girls.

Relationships among women and girls are well described by the Greek term *koinonia,* which refers to "the relationships experienced by Christians with God, Jesus Christ, the Holy Spirit, and among themselves in the early church."[3] Acts 2:42–47 describes life among members of the early church as being devoted to the apostles' teaching, sharing meals, praying together, and sharing in material possessions according to the needs of the community. Such settings of intellectual, pious, and physical interaction yield a spiritual intimacy among members of a community that is understood as communion. The point of the sharing among members of the community is not to be self-serving, nor is it solely for the edification of the members, but it is for God. *Koinonia* signifies the ultimate nature of relationships expressed in common values, beliefs, and goals while simultaneously valuing the uniqueness of individuals. Later in this chapter I will argue that the femaleship among women and girls is like the communion of women with each other and with God. But I begin by illustrating femaleship.

The relationship between twelve-year-old Nel Wright and Sula Peace in Toni Morrison's *Sula* demonstrates the nature of fellowship that is akin to communion. The girls' relationship was innocent and fiercely loyal. From ages twelve to seventeen, Nel and Sula were inseparable, sharing secrets as well as hopes and dreams.[4] Their childhood relationship as little black girls who authentically communed stands in contrast to the break in their relationship as adult women when Nel discovers her husband is having an affair with Sula. The nature of their relationship when they were young girls offers clues about communion that arises through innocence and loyalty. The kind of innocence we see in the relationship between Nel and Sula is chaste and undefiled by distrust. Friendship that is innocent is completely void of evil intent, deception, and guile. Toni Morrison helps define the innocence that Nel and Sula embody as she describes Nel's skill at preparing a twig to be a tool

3. McKim, *Westminster Dictionary of Theological Terms,* 154.

4. Morrison, *Sula,* 52.

for digging a cup-shaped hole in the ground during a moment of "grass play" between Nel and Sula.[5] Morrison writes: "Nel found a thick twig and, with her thumbnail, pulled away its bark until it was stripped to a smooth, creamy innocence."[6] Sula copied Nel's process and "undressed" a twig for her use.[7] Morrison's description of Nel and Sula's activity implies that the innocence that the girls share is pure and unblemished yet covered by the "bark" of being female, black, and poor. Innocence is an ontological state reflected in the lives and intimate friendships of little black girls.

Innocence is coupled with loyalty, such as the unconditional loyalty that Nel and Sula shared. When they were both twelve during the summer of 1922, the girls developed a fondness for "beautiful black boys."[8] They would follow them down to the river and watch them swim. On a hot day that July, a little boy they called Chicken Little came up from the lower bank of the river where the girls were playing. Sula and Nel teased Chicken for picking his nose and eating the buggers. Sula coaxed him into climbing a tall tree and joined him to survey the vastness of the river, then coaxed the reluctant Chicken back down the tree. Then

> Sula picked him up by his hands and swung him outward then around and around. His knickers ballooned and his shrieks of frightened joy startled the birds and the fat grasshoppers. When he slipped from her hand and sailed away out over the water they could still hear his bubbly laughter.
>
> The water darkened and closed quickly over the place where Chicken Little sank. The pressure of his hand and tight little fingers were still in Sula's palms as she stood looking at the closed place in the water. They expected him to come back up, laughing. Both stared at the water.[9]

5. Ibid., 58.
6. Ibid.
7. Ibid.
8. Ibid., 56.
9. Ibid., 60–61.

The first words spoken were Nel's: she wondered whether anyone had seen what had happened. Sula ran to see whether anyone in the only house nearby had witnessed the accident. The owner of the house, Shadrack—a shell-shocked war veteran—offered no decisive response that he knew anything. Over the four days that Chicken's body was missing, the girls, loyal to each other, told no one about the accident. A bargeman found Chicken's body. During his funeral Sula and Nel sang in the church's junior choir. Nel was filled with fear that their deed would be discovered. Overcome with fear and regret, Sula cried throughout the funeral. The girls held hands and stood at a distance as they watched the small casket being lowered into the ground. Yet they never told anyone else what had really happened to Chicken and what their role had been. The secret was theirs, sealed in the bonds of their loyalty to each other. Loyalty and innocence, as illustrated in the friendship between Nel and Sula, are essential twin characteristics for femaleship that leads to communion.

Femaleship in Mixing Nia

The movie *Mixing Nia* likewise explores femaleship as communion among friends. Nia Evans, a black/white mixed-race co-ed is the central protagonist who struggles to find her true identity. Her quest is set into motion when her boss at a prominent New York advertising firm asks her to write an ad campaign for malt liquor targeting black kids. Outraged, Nia quits her job and attempts to write a novel about historical aspects of African Americans. Eventually, she writes a novel that incorporates truths from her life experiences as the daughter of an African American woman and a white Jewish man and her maternal and fraternal ancestors' plight in North America. While self-discovery involves a number of Nia's interpersonal relationships, a focus on her relationship with her best girlfriends illustrates femaleship. Nia's relationships with Renee, who is black, and Jen, who is white, reveal the real and raw nature of fellowship.

Early in the movie, we see Nia walking between her two clos-est college friends as she shares her decision to leave the advertis-ing firm because she felt it unethical to target poor young black youth in the inner city with ads for Slam Beer. Jen and Renee both affirm that Nia's moral compass steered her in the right direction but alert her to the reality of life without employment. Nia assures her girlfriends that she has savings that will keep her comfortable for at least two months. Nia explains that she wants to write a novel and reminds them that she has demonstrated her writing ability while in college. Renee and Jen both candidly comment that Nia's writing ability is not such that she will be able to earn money by it yet. Their candid response stops Nia in her tracks and both Jen and Renee walk together ahead of Nia without recanting their critical and candid advice.

The next scene shows Renee accompanying Nia to a writ-ers' workshop, which apparently Renee encouraged Nia to attend given her obvious determination to become a writer. Nia's resis-tance to writing lessons is overheard by the professor prior to his lecture, yet she is drawn into his inspiring lecture and finds herself attracted to him. She leaves Lewis, the professor, a phone message. He returns her call and soon becomes her intimate partner. Renee befriends Lewis through her relationship with Nia and accompa-nies them on several occasions.

During a wedding dress fitting for Jen, who asks Nia to be a bridesmaid in her forthcoming wedding, Jen asks Nia for advice. Jen starts to cry as she explains that she feels ugly in all the wed-ding dresses that she tries on and that she is sure she will not look beautiful to her fiancé as she walks down the aisle. Nia consoles Jen, who stops crying and asks Nia what is wrong with her. Jen states that Nia looks drawn and thin, that she never sees Nia any-more, and that she misses their routine visits. It becomes clear that Jen is more concerned about her relationship with Nia than her own anxieties about her upcoming wedding. Nia complains about Lewis and notes a concern that Renee is always around when she is out with Lewis. Jen explains that Renee is just lonely and that Nia should introduce her to other men.

Nia therefore introduces Renee to her white former coworker, Matt, whom she dated prior to meeting Lewis. The four double-date at an event, then Matt and Renee leave Nia and Lewis and go dancing. Renee finds that Matt lacks sex appeal, and frankly indicates she is not into dating white guys. She tells Nia and Lewis about the events of the previous night and how she left Matt dancing, though he was unaware that she had walked away. Nia tells Renee how rude she was to abandon Matt without saying good night.

As time goes by Nia suspects Renee is interested in Lewis and she becomes insecure. Nia's relationship with Lewis becomes more and more strained as he chides her for not embracing her black identity. They break up after a heated argument and she seeks affection once again from Matt. While she swings between her two primary dating relationships, her neighbor, Joe, seems to understand her the most, yet she does not view him as a viable intimate partner, just as a friend.

Confused about her own identity, she telephones Lewis out of desperation the night before Jen's wedding. Renee answers Lewis's phone and innocently passes it to Lewis. He speaks briefly with Nia, then rushes over to her apartment to comfort her. Nia feels her friend has betrayed her by dating Lewis. He explains that Renee only answered the phone in anticipation that a friend of hers was returning her phone call. Lewis continues justifying Renee's visit as being purely out of their mutual interest in her welfare, but convinces Nia how deeply he cares for her and spends the night with her. The next day Lewis assures Nia that he will be at the wedding and rushes home to get dressed. Matt also calls and also reassures Nia he will be at the wedding. Flustered, Nia dresses and rushes out to hail a taxi to the wedding dressed in her lavender bridesmaid's dress. She arrives late, just as the bridesmaids are lining up to enter the church sanctuary, and apologizes to Jen, who graciously tells her not to worry. As Nia proceeds into church, she acknowledges both Lewis and Matt sitting in the pews and they notice each other. They confront Nia immediately after the wedding ceremony, debating why she should choose one of them. Jen delays the wedding party from leaving without Nia. Renee stands nearby watching the triangular debate between Lewis, Nia, and Matt. Nia finally tells Matt and Lewis she is not interested in either of them. Matt walks away with a look of defeat. Lewis steps over to Renee, who rejects him with a hand gesture in his face, and he walks away. At that moment Nia realizes that Renee was never personally interested in Lewis. Then Jen beckons Nia to get into the waiting limousine with the wedding party so they can travel to the wedding reception.

As Renee and Nia are leaving the reception, Renee assures her that she would never compromise their long-standing friendship, that she never had a romantic interest in Lewis. Renee and Nia embrace before Renee gestures toward her date waiting for her. After Renee leaves, Nia fails to hail a taxi, so she runs home in hopes of talking with her neighbor Joe. But Joe had moved the previous day for a six-month job in California and has sublet his apartment to a female tenant. The movie ends with Nia reading the closing paragraph of her newly published book to an audience in an "open mic" setting with Joe there supporting her with applause.

Renee and Jen, in their own unique ways, demonstrate friendship that is loyal and honest. Both women accompanied Nia on her journey to discover her true identity even though the journey had some difficult moments that tested the strength of their bond. Renee gently accompanied Nia while she came to terms with her black identity, whereas Lewis pushed Nia to discover her black identity. Renee was patient with Nia and always careful to tell her the truth about her observations and her own desires for intimacy with a male partner. Renee symbolized the "beautiful character" of the black female that was juxtaposed to Nia's mother, who, also a black female, was typecast as the "ugly character." Renee was loyal to Nia even when Nia could not recognize Renee's loyalty, particularly when Nia was suspicious that Renee was involved with Lewis. It became apparent that Renee had been loyal to Nia all along, listening to both Nia and Lewis during a tenuous time in their relationship.

Jen symbolizes the "beautiful character" of the white person juxtaposed with Nia's father who was also white and typecast as a white self-absorbed womanizer of young women. Like Renee, Jen demonstrated loyalty and patience with Nia as she searched for her identity. Jen found ways to make Nia aware of her choices and behavior that were inconsistent with her true self without berating or accusing her. Both Renee (black) and Jen (white) helped mirror to Nia the best of who she was as a black/white mixed-race person. They also modeled loyalty, understood as unconditional faithfulness, among women of different races/ethnicities, and complete commitment to the well-being of Nia. This form of women's loyalty and the reflection of "beautiful character" are the essence of femaleship.

Femaleship in *The Girl Who Fell from the Sky*

We see this same femaleship characterized as "beautiful character" epitomized between an aunt and her niece in Heidi Durrow's novel, *The Girl Who Fell from the Sky*. Its protagonist, Rachel Morse, is a black/white mixed-race girl who has survived a suicide/murder when her mother, Nella, pushed her brother off the roof of a building and then jumped to her death with Rachel's baby sister in her arms, after also attempting to push Rachel off the roof. Rachel jumped after her mother and siblings in an attempt to catch her brother's hand but landed on top of him.[10] Although hospitalized in serious condition from her fall, the only permanent damage she suffered was hearing loss in one ear. Her fraternal grandmother, Doris, and fraternal aunt, Loretta, who take her in after the tragic deaths of her Danish mother and two siblings, are key female relationships in Rachel's life. While she longs to live with her father, a technical sergeant in the US Air Force, he has placed her in the care of his mother and sister. Rachel is eleven years old when she comes to live with her Grandmother Doris and Aunt Loretta. Rachel struggles with racial identity, stereotypes, physical

---

10. Durrow, *The Girl Who Fell from The Sky*, 238.

appearance, and her sexuality. As she comes of age, she longs for Mor, an affectionate Danish name for her mother, to care for her as only a loving mother can. She compares Mor with Grandmother Doris. Grandma Doris is stern, authoritative, and opinionated. She is usually angry except when she is gardening.[11] When Grandma Doris starts to fuss, Rachel states, "I have a trick figured out . . . so I don't make mean thoughts about her. . . . Thoughts like she's not so smart, like she's not as good a mother as Mor."[12] As the novel progresses we learn that Mor struggled with domestic violence at the hands of Rachel's father and her mother's boyfriend, who is also the father of her baby. Rachel's Mor had spiraled down into depression because of racial slurs hurled at her biracial children and the poverty they experience. Yet, to Rachel, Mor is the ideal mother when compared with Grandma Doris.

Rachel also compares and contrasts her Aunt Loretta to Grandma Doris. Unlike the comparison between Mor and Grandma Doris, Aunt Loretta is not a mother type but the ideal embodiment of beauty in both character and appearance. Rachel is careful to compare the skin color of her grandmother and her aunt to her own. Grandma is eggplant brown[13] and Aunt Loretta is nut brown.[14] Rachel states, "I want to be a beautiful Aunt Loretta. She smiles all the time. . . . Her teeth are white like paper and straight. She shows her teeth when she smiles. I have a cover-up-my teeth smile."[15] Aunt Loretta is pretty, a good tennis player, smart, and she has class.[16] She was once married to a basketball player, Nathan, who took her to visit New York City where, among other things, she went to museums and art galleries. At one point in her life Rachel had worked up the nerve to show some of her own art, but that possibility was dashed when she discovered Nathan was being

11. Ibid., 32.
12. Ibid., 33.
13. Ibid., 4.
14. Ibid., 7.
15. Ibid., 6–7.
16. Ibid., 29, 33.

unfaithful.[17] She divorced Nathan and moved back to Portland to live with her mother.

Aunt Loretta cares for Rachel, but not like her Mor did. Aunt Loretta brushes her hair each morning and cooks her pancakes for breakfast. Rachel makes the telling distinction, "I feel like a boxer getting ready to fight in the ring. Not tender, just taken care of."[18]

Aunt Loretta is the voice of reason and sound advice. When Tamika, one of the African American girls at school, bullies Rachel after she straightens her long hair, Aunt Loretta tells Rachel Tamika is just jealous because her own hair won't grow. Regarding Tamika's jealously, Aunt Loretta says, "You make them work harder."[19] Aunt Loretta is the voice of wisdom and reason. She has a kind of beauty and confidence that Rachel admires and seeks to emulate as the new girl at school.

When Aunt Loretta and Drew, the man she dates, take Rachel to Multnomah Falls, the experience is transformative for Rachel and her aunt. After climbing to the top of the stairs to observe the waterfall, they discover that the cold winter air has frozen the water into spectacular icicles cascading down the side of the mountain. Noticing her aunt staring out at the waterfall and framing it in the air as if preparing to paint what she sees, Rachel comments, "Aunt Loretta is leaning on the rail, looking at the waterfall now. She's hypnotized. I think she is crying."[20] Rachel watches Drew embrace her aunt and Rachel barely hears her say, "I want to be that girl again."[21] Days later Aunt Loretta has a new form of beauty: she is now painting again. The beauty of the waterfall inspired Aunt Loretta to create beautiful images once more. She finds beauty in almost everything: in leaves, pebbles, wrappers, and peels from which she makes things.[22] While she has always decorated herself, she now also decorates the house, replacing browns with African

17. Ibid., 55.
18. Ibid., 11.
19. Ibid., 68.
20. Ibid., 76.
21. Ibid.
22. Ibid., 77.

brown fabric, Rachel notes.[23] Aunt Loretta has even begun to teach
Rachel about Africa and her African heritage as she decorates the
house with photographs of African people. She has also dug out an
easel, paints, and paint cloth from the basement trunks, much to
the dismay of Grandma Doris, who feels Aunt Loretta will never
get a man if she has paint under her fingernails.[24] Nevertheless,
Aunt Loretta paints all sorts of pictures of the waterfall, animals,
and Rachel's profile. As Rachel sits for her portrait, Aunt Loretta
talks about Rachel's father and mother and how her father's former
girlfriends looked, and when he will return.[25] Aunt Loretta always
refers to Rachel with kind and affectionate words, calling her "my
sweet" in reply to her queries.[26]

Aunt Loretta eventually moves in with Drew but continues
to visit Rachel twice a week. Rachel comments, "I wish she had
taken me too."[27] Struggles over how a respectable girl should look
at school or church have intensified between Rachel and Grandma
Doris since Aunt Loretta moved away. Grandma has also insisted
that Rachel join the choir. One Sunday when she doesn't sing in
the choir, Rachel agrees to wear the yellow dress and matching
shoes that grandma bought at the Saint Vincent de Paul thrift store
for fifty cents. After adjusting her look with a sweater, Rachel comments on her new appearance:

> If you ask me I would say that mostly I don't look like
> myself when I wear church finery. Or feel like a self that
> makes any sense. And today my scalp itches because
> Grandma made me go to the hairdresser to get me look-
> ing more respectable. "None of those people want to see
> a pickaninny in the church," Grandma said. She is glad
> that my hair has grown out again. I can't say that I don't
> like the way my hair looks. It's straight now—straight like
> Mor's hair for the first time ever. And it's long enough for

23. Ibid., 77–78.
24. Ibid., 78.
25. Ibid., 79.
26. Ibid., 80.
27. Ibid., 97.

me to move it off my shoulder with a swish. But the hair-
dresser let the relaxer set too long and burned a few spots
on my scalp and burned my left ear with the blow-dryer's
hot metal tip. And I am still tender-headed.[28]

Wearing straight hair has been a dangerous enterprise at
school for Rachel. Two weeks earlier, she had worn her hair straight
to school and the girls who hang out in the bathroom questioned
whether her long straight hair was authentically hers or a weave.
Now with Rachel's straight hair pulled back to show the full frame
of her face, people have noticed she looks different. Rachel comments, "I look pretty."[29] That prettiness is a combination of her
mother's blue eyes and straight hair. Even her science teacher, Mr.
Barucci, said she "looked very beautiful, a pure masterpiece. . . .
Makes those eyes more startling to look at." Throwing a kiss into
the air he concluded, "Bella!"[30]

Aunt Loretta and Drew had dropped by while Rachel and
her grandmother were preparing for church. Observing her aunt's
carefree and happy aura, Rachel, now fourteen and about to enter
high school, romanticizes how she will be like Aunt Loretta, walking out on a Sunday morning with her boyfriend by her side. She
imagines achieving straight *As* in high school, going to college, and
then seeing the world. She concludes, "I guess I'll be someone like
Aunt Loretta a black woman—the kind of woman I will be."[31] As
Aunt Loretta backs out the door with Drew close behind, Rachel
observes her tennis bag on her shoulder, her painted fingernails,
and the sparkly engagement ring on her finger. With words of regret that Rachel can't go with her, Aunt Loretta calls her "sweet"
as if Rachel is candy. Her aunt's words imply a promise to see her
soon.

The fate of that Sunday could not have been predicted. While
Rachel and Grandma Doris participated in worship, Aunt Loretta tripped on her shoelace and landed on a piece of glass on

28. Ibid., 96.
29. Ibid., 97.
30. Ibid.
31. Ibid., 98.

the public tennis court. Grandma Doris receives the phone call while listening to the Gospel, and instinctively cries out, "Oh good Lord . . . she cut her face." Trying to calm her grandma, Rachel responds, "At least she didn't poke out an eye."[32] Yet Rachel imagined her beautiful aunt's smile with a jagged slice in it held together by long sewing stitches. "And her hands covering up her smile, so she won't make Grandma mad looking at the now ugly ex-Rose Festival princess."[33] Grandma Doris will not allow Rachel to go to the hospital. She sits alone praying, without knowing how to lift up her aunt.

Two months later Aunt Loretta is still hospitalized and Rachel has not seen her. Drew helps Rachel sneak into the hospital and offers to accompany her, but she prefers to go in alone. While Aunt Loretta does indeed have a ragged scar on her face, the cause of her sickness is due to an allergic reaction to the antibiotics she was given. Rachel bravely enters the hospital, washes her hands, and puts on gloves, a gown, and a mask. During this process she practices smiling and saying "I love you" in the mirror over the sink before she enters her aunt's room.[34] When Rachel enters Aunt Loretta's hospital room she sees rolling poles and machines with tubes that run under her aunt's bed sheet. There is a tube in her aunt's mouth that "keeps away her smile."[35] She is happy her aunt is sleeping because it means she can't see Rachel cry. The mask hides Rachel's well-rehearsed smile. Aunt Loretta's swollen face is held together with thread covered with sticky brown blood. Her tiny arms are swollen. The places where Aunt Loretta's skin is coming off reveal "giant white patches where she used to be brown."[36] Rachel imagines the "whiteness beautiful. Not hot and raw . . . . Like giant burns."[37] She imagines her aunt will become the color of porcelain like the figures in Grandma's cupboard; she will become

32. Ibid., 100.
33. Ibid.
34. Ibid., 101.
35. Ibid.
36. Ibid., 102.
37. Ibid.

special. "She will be the perfect color for jewels and long gloves and worship."[38] After Aunt Loretta's death, Rachel reflects on her passing in contrast to others' deaths. Instead of getting sick and going away like other people who die, Aunt Loretta, Rachel says, opened a door that "last Sunday morning I saw her with her light on."[39]

Aunt Loretta was a symbol of beauty to Rachel. Her aunt embodied imagination, possibility, gentleness, and care, and her physical appearance was that of a beautiful black woman. She was also a surrogate mother for Rachel. At the point of her death, Rachel had begun to appreciate her more and more. Aunt Loretta modeled true womanhood through her sexuality and spirituality. She embodied hope that liberated Rachel from her painful past of seeing her mother abused by men rather than being honored and adored like Drew did Aunt Loretta. Drew demonstrated love that helped Loretta "turn her light on" again to pursue happiness. Even though death intervened before their engagement could lead to marriage, Drew continued to care for Rachel and Grandma Doris like a faithful uncle/son-in-law. Because of how Aunt Loretta modeled womanhood, now fourteen-year-old Rachel not only knows that she is black,[40] but embraces her racial identity while she struggles for a wholesome relationship with her grandmother and other teenaged girls at school and church.

Femaleship as Communion with God

Femaleship among girlfriends and aunts, as illustrated in the books and movie discussed above, approximates communion with God. The term *fellowship*, described here as femaleship, captures the notion of communion as a deep level of companionship, intimacy, and friendship.[41] The femaleship that we saw exemplified

38. Ibid.
39. Ibid.
40. Ibid., 20.
41. "Fellowship," http://dictionary.reference.com/browse/fellowship.

in the fictional characters of Nia and Rachel is loyal and honest accompaniment and an example of beauty. Femaleship is also a sign of innocence, as we saw in the relationship between Nel and Sula. Such communion among women and girls that includes innocence, loyalty, and honesty, resembles and reveals communion with God, especially when race and gender simultaneously obfuscate wholesome female relationships.

The beautiful qualities of communion among biracial/mixed-race women are not salvific attributes for problems of racism and sexism, but a prism of possibilities through which mixed-race women and women of all racial/ethnic backgrounds can innocently receive each other without conditions. Their innocence of reception is void of presuppositions and hermeneutics of suspicion. Mixed-race women and other women receive each other with the innocence of little girls who develop deep friendships in which they are completely exposed to each other. Their trust in each other is uncompromising. The lives of two little girls meet, unbiased by years of experience of human failure that makes them cautious of each other. They are vulnerable like the friendship between Nel and Sula in Toni Morrison's novel. This is the type of innocence that mixed-race women must exemplify if their lives are to have a divine quality of communion. However, along with their innocence they must have the knowledge of the truth of racial and gender injustice, yet they must strive not to let that knowledge impede their relationships—their femaleship—with one another.

As important as is innocence of reception, the beautiful quality of loyalty among biracial/mixed-race women supersedes innocence. First, mixed-race women must be loyal to their own biological and psychosocial identity as women born into a society in which the social construction of race renders them as anomalies. Mixed-race women must not falter to be all they are regardless of societal prescriptions and pressures to choose the supposedly more superior race (white) and deny the inferior race (black) and the perceived advantages of being a white female rather than a black female. Self-loyalty for the mixed-race woman means rejecting such racist and sexist proscriptions and embracing both her black and white female identity. Second, once self-loyalty is achieved, the mixed-race woman can be authentically loyal to other women.

Loyalty for the mixed-race woman is thus joined to honesty with self and with other women. Honesty is righteous truth-telling about prejudices against dark-skin–colored women and accompanying stereotypes in a racially divided society. Mixed-race women, regardless of whether their skin color is dark brown or light (almost white), must be forthright and honest about physical biases against black women. Integrity is in short supply with regards to the problem of racism and sexism in North American society. Honesty modeled by mixed-race women would advance the cause of race and gender justice in a society that desperately needs it. As indicated above, the beautiful qualities of communion among biracial/mixed-race women that is innocent, loyal, and honest approximates communion with God. Such communion is a foretaste of emancipatory hope—a liberative hope that expects God to transform oppressive situations and affirms human agency in ushering in God's vision of transformation.

Femaleship captures the notion of *koinonia* or communion among women that brings about unity of all humankind rooted in love. Women who practice such unity with one another point to an ultimate and deeper intimacy of communion with God; together, these can bridge the chasm of racism, sexism, and patriarchy.

Using Acts 2:42, 44–47 as the biblical framework for the educational curriculum of a church community, Maria Harris writes about such communion in her book *Fashion Me a People*. She argues for *koinonia*, community and communion, as one of five forms that are the core of educational ministry in a congregation. Harris insists that people seek communities of faith that will satisfy their deep longing for unity of all humankind.[42] Thus, the burden of a Christian community is to become one and to be rooted in love, as expressed in the New Testament, so that the longing for unity/oneness is our common aspiration.[43] Communion within

42. Harris, *Fashion Me A People*, 76.
43. Ibid., 77.

Christian community aims at "overcoming brokenness, and ultimately toward achieving wholeness."[44] Such communion, whether in the church or in society, is communion with God.

44. Ibid.

3

Fortitude

FORTITUDE IS THE INTELLECTUAL and spiritual strength to persevere even in the midst of seemingly insurmountable odds. It requires courage, patience, and perseverance. Fortitude is "mental and emotional strength in facing difficulty, adversity, danger, or temptation courageously."[1] When systemic societal practices veil possibilities for living a wholesome life, women with fortitude press relentlessly toward possibilities for a wholesome life. With unwavering determination and courage, black women with fortitude "make a way out of no way." This chapter examines such fortitude in the mulatta and her tragic relationships with other women, for fortitude is a scaffold for emancipatory hope.

Harriet Tubman, Fannie Lou Hamer, Maya Angelou, and a host of other African American women are well-known examples of those who demonstrated fortitude from the enslavement period through the civil rights movement. In addition to these women, there were young female activists coming of age who gave shape to the events of the movement. The fortitude of Ruby Doris Smith and Diane Nash of the Student Nonviolent Coordinating Committee (SNCC) never wavered during their involvement in the civil rights movement. Nash, a student at Fisk University, led the Nashville students. Smith, a seventeen-year-old student at Spelman College,

---

1. "Fortitude," http://dictionary.reference.com/brose/fortitude?s.

led students in Atlanta. These young women were independent, courageous, confident, emotionally and mentally strong, and intellectually brilliant. Nash and Smith, along with SNCC members Charles Sherrod and Charles Jones, became known for their "jail, no bail" strategy during the "sit-ins" to desegregate lunch counters.[2] Students from the NAACP and CORE in Rock Hill, South Carolina who were arrested and jailed after attending a CORE workshop then implemented this new strategy in an effort to conserve resources. After the first round of arrests, CORE asked for help and Nash, Smith, Sherrod, and Jones came in and were jailed for thirty days without bail. The month of incarceration brought "hard labor, fragile health, and racial indignities" that resulted in a chronic stomach ailment for Smith.[3] Yet the tenacity of the four students earned them the moniker "the Rock Hill Four." During a demonstration in Mississippi, Nash was arrested. Though she was pregnant when she was subsequently jailed, she refused to appeal her conviction and remained in jail. She wrote:

> We in the nonviolent movement have been talking about jail without bail for two years or more . . . . The time has come for us to mean what we say and stop posting bond. . . . This will be a Black baby born in Mississippi and thus, wherever he is born, he will be born in prison. I believe that if I go to jail now it may help hasten that day when my child and all children will be free—not only on the day of their birth but for all their lives.[4]

Diane Nash resolved to practice the "jail, no bail" tactic regardless of her physical condition. Her fortitude was paralleled only by a few other SNCC young women.

One such woman was Ruby Doris Smith. She too was incarcerated in some of the most deplorable and inhuman prisons in the South, including the Parchman State Penitentiary in Mississippi, and she too practiced the "jail, no bail" tactic. During the events of the freedom rides through Mississippi, over 300 volunteers were

2. Giddings, *When and Where I Enter*, 278.

3. Ibid., 278.

4. Ibid., 279.

54

arrested in Jackson.[5] Ruby and other students were sentenced to a two-month jail term. Mississippi law authorities determined that Jackson's Hinds County Jail was insufficient for the large number of young SNCC volunteers and proceeded to move some of the inmates to Parchman State Penitentiary. Ruby and the other students were awakened at 4:00 AM and packed inside a poorly ventilated truck in hot summer temperatures. Their anxiety and fear mounted as they realized "it would be easy for their racist prison guards to execute them here in rural Mississippi and bury their bodies where nobody would ever find them."[6] Conditions at Parchman Prison were deplorable. Upon arrival, all their clothes and shoes were removed and all their body cavities searched. The cells were filthy and filled with bugs. In an effort to silence the students' singing and talking, the prison guards then confiscated "their mattresses, towels, sheets, and toothbrushes."[7] Although Ruby and a few other women were moved "to the prison infirmary in an effort to relieve overcrowding in the cell block,"[8] the conditions there were only slightly better. From the infirmary window, Ruby witnessed scenes much like those at the time of actual slavery: she saw approximately sixty black men working under deadly conditions guarded by one white man brandishing a rifle and seated on a white horse.[9] The two-month incarceration in Parchman Prison brought moments of deep reflection and transformation for Ruby and the student volunteers, and united the disparate activists into one movement.

The "jail, no bail" campaign certainly showcased Ruby's fortitude as a rising leader in SNCC, but that fortitude was a quality she had already shown early in her activist career. During the Atlanta boycotts in 1960, the eighteen-year-old Ruby had participated in picket lines, marches, and sit-ins. When the A & P grocery store

5. Fleming, *Soon We Will Not Cry*, 85.
6. Ibid., 86.
7. Ibid., 87.
8. Ibid.
9. Ibid.

was the target of protests, Ruby was "the only person marching around and carrying a picket sign in front of the store":[10]

> Walking back and forth in front of the A & P, Ruby ached for the camaraderie. In the midst of her discomfort, though, she discovered a strength deep inside herself, an unshakable commitment to the cause of civil rights that kept her coming back day after day when there was no publicity, no one to march with her and bolster her courage, and almost no recognition of her activity from her own community.[11]

Despite the humidity of the hot Atlanta summer and the deadly southern racist environment, she stayed the course, many times courageously picketing stores alone.

 She was also active in the kneel-ins during that Atlanta summer of 1960. Buoyed by her theological formation in the Christian Methodist Episcopal Church, she was disconcerted by the racist attitudes in the white churches. She "expected Christian moral ethics to soften the heart of even the staunchest segregationist."[12] During a lone attempt to desegregate a white church, the ushers blocked Ruby from entering the sanctuary. Some white congregants stared directly at Ruby during the disruption in the narthex, while others refused to look at her, as though she didn't exist. While the looks made her want to scream "But this is the Lord's house!" she refused to leave. Ruby reported: "I pulled up a chair in the lobby and joined in the singing and the worship services which I enjoyed immensely."[13] An article in the *Atlanta Inquirer* reported an interview with Ruby in which she commented on the success of the kneel-in movement, even her one lone attempt. She felt that the "minds and hearts of people who turned the [activists] [a]way were undoubtedly stirred."[14] Her comments indicated her hope that there could be a solution to segregation and racial injustice.

10. Ibid., 55.
11. Ibid., 56.
12. Ibid.
13. Ibid.
14. Ibid.

Ruby and Diane were two of many young women in the SNCC whose fortitude ensured the success of the civil rights movement.

The ballet *Cry*, choreographed by Alvin Ailey, captured artistically the fortitude of black women like Ruby Doris Smith and Diane Nash. In his autobiography he wrote that *Cry* was dedicated to his mother, Mrs. Lula Elizabeth Cooper, and black women everywhere.[15] Mrs. Cooper was a single mother of her only child, Alvin. She worked extremely hard to provide for her son and herself as a domestic and field hand in Texas, their home state. She was the first black woman employee in the Navasota Hospital. She spent much of her time searching for better jobs, and meanwhile had to leave Alvin with family members or acquaintances.[16] When she was twenty-six and Alvin was seven she moved to Los Angeles and became one of the first black "Rosie the Riveters" on the midnight shift of the Lockheed Aircraft Industry.[17] When she had saved enough money to provide a home, food, and clothing for Alvin, she sent for him to join her.[18] In addition to her ethic of hard work and provision for her child, her test of strength in the midst of adversity and danger occurred during a situation that most women could not survive. Ailey wrote:

> When I was about five years old, my mother was raped by four white men. She never admitted to me that it happened. She only recently found out that I knew about it. One night she didn't come home until ten P.M. She usually came home at three or four in the afternoon. She probably had been working in some white people's kitchen. That was the other kind of work, along with picking cotton, available to black people. It was very clear to me that my mother was crying. She had bruises all over her body. I don't think she ever told anyone about it except maybe her sisters or friends from church. I kept quiet and pretended I was asleep the whole time.[19]

15. Ailey, with Bailey, *Revelations*, 129.
16. Ibid., 25.
17. Ibid., 32.
18. Ibid., 31–33.
19. Ibid., 19.

Rape is an egregious crime against the body and mind of any woman. Gang rape motivated by racist beliefs that black women are less than human and therefore created for white male aggression and sexual lust is a particular heinous crime against black women. Mrs. Cooper persevered with strength of mind and will while bearing the scars and the memory of being raped by four white men.

His mother was the "text" from which Alvin Ailey created the ballet *Cry*. He choreographed the ballet as a birthday gift for her in 1971. "It's a tribute to black women's history through images of struggle in an abstract way."[20] Ailey indicates that the three-part ballet begins with slavery and servitude, is followed by rage and anger, and concludes with joyfulness. The ballet, first performed by Judith Jamison in 1971, reveals strength, struggle, courage, and triumphant joy as key characteristics of fortitude among black women.[21]

Birdie Lee, the narrator and protagonist in *Caucasia*,[22] a novel by Danzy Senna, embodies precisely such fortitude. It evolves as she comes of age during the civil rights movement amid a disastrous life of familial color prejudice, societal racial injustice, divorced parents, a fugitive life, and passing as white. Born in 1967, Birdie was the second daughter of Sandra, her white mother, and Deck, her black father. Sandra Lodge Lee grew up in Cambridge, the daughter of a Harvard professor and a socialite mother who were both descendants of old Boston families.[23] Deck grew up in Roxbury with his sister Dot, his only living family member. He and Sandy met in Harvard Square when Deck, a doctoral student, and two other students who were accompanying her father, a professor of classics, gathered for conversation about his paper in the class on Plato and Aristotle.[24] Sandy and Deck took note of each other that evening through his acknowledgement of her intellectual

20. Alvin Ailey interview, ArtHaus Musik, 1986.
21. Ibid.
22. Senna, *Caucasia*.
23. Ibid., 7 and 24.
24. Ibid., 33.

ability to read Albert Camus's diary as an eighteen-year-old and her wonder about this African American man. He disrupted all the stereotypes she knew of black people, particularly their alleged simplemindedness. Sandy and Deck were married on the Cambridge lawn of Professor and Mrs. Lodge during the tumultuous time of the sixties amid "riots and race wars" in Boston.[25] Their union produced two girls. First in 1964 was Cole, short for Colette, and then Birdie.

Cole proved Birdie's existence.[26] Birdie said, "That face was me and I was that face."[27] Before Birdie saw herself, she saw her beloved older sister, Cole, and imagined that her own face was the reflection of Cole's "cinnamon-skinned, curly-haired" face.[28] Cole had kinky hair and a small round nose like their father's and eyes the color of "sea glass, forever shifting between blue, green, and gray."[29] During the summer, Cole's skin would turn honey-colored, but in the winter her skin color was closer to Birdie's shade of beige.[30] When washed and combed with hair oil from the African/ ethnic hair products section of the drug store, Cole's hair framed her face in black ringlets. Birdie's skin color of beige suggested she was Sicilian.[31] Only in the summertime did her skin color darken to Cole's cinnamon color. Birdie's hair was straight, more the color of her mother's blonde hair, and her features were pointed like those of Europeans. Even though Birdie as a toddler believed she was a reflection of Cole, outsiders never perceived them as sisters.

Nevertheless, Birdie and Cole's sisterly love shone forth as unconditional companionship. In their cloistered bedroom in the attic of their Brownstone home in the South End of Boston, they played dress up as well as make believe and shared secrets. They

25. Ibid., 39.
26. Ibid., 5.
27. Ibid.
28. Ibid.
29. Ibid., 43.
30. Ibid., 42–43.
31. Ibid., 27.

spoke their own language, Elemeno,[32] to communicate with each other in their bedroom as well as in the presence of adults and other children. Cole insisted that Elemeno began when Birdie was still in their mother's womb and Cole was only three years old. She would place her forehead on their "mother's belly and tell secrets to Birdie in her three-year-old gibberish genius, all the while using her finger to trace a kind of invisible hieroglyphics against [their] mother's swollen flesh."[33] Cole believed Birdie was lonely and frightened of the dark and that her voice and scribblings would be comforting. The sisters alone spoke Elemeno; their mother and father could not understand the language, and it so alarmed their maternal grandmother that she advocated that the girls see a child psychiatrist.

Cole protected Birdie with fierce courage. Homeschooled by their mother, at ages eleven and eight they started attending the Nkrumah School in Roxbury, which had an Afrocentric curriculum. School administrators and students alike received Cole as black but not Birdie. Students referred to Birdie as [Puerto] "Rican" or something unidentifiable and taunted her with spitballs.[34] Some wanted to know whether she was white. School girls would bully Birdie when she was isolated from teachers and Cole. One such occasion occurred in the second-floor girls' room where Birdie was harassed by Maria Miller, "a pretty girl with thick black hair and smooth brown skin."[35] Maria and three other girls waited outside the bathroom stall until Birdie had finished using the toilet. When she was washing her hands Maria stepped behind her and slowly reached over her head and suddenly yanked her ponytail. In a sneering voice Maria said, "Why you so stuck up? You think you're fine?"[36] Pulling Birdie's hair back towards her, Maria commanded Cathy Murphy, who was tall and yellow complexioned, to move close and said, "She thinks she's all that just 'cause she got long,

32. Ibid., 47.
33. Ibid.
34. Ibid., 43.
35. Ibid., 45.
36. Ibid., 46.

stringy hair. I say we give Ms. Thang a makeover." [37] Maria's intent was motivated by her perception that Ali, a boy who repeatedly asked Birdie whether she was white, was rejecting her for Birdie. "You think Ali's gonna like you when you don't got no hair?"[38] she teased. Another girl, Cherise, was commanded to get some scissors but she refused. Chiding Cherise, Cathy fetched the scissors from the arts classroom herself while Birdie's ponytail remained in Maria's tight grasp. Birdie closed her eyes and anticipated the limp ponytail swinging in Maria's hand as she listened to the swift slice of the scissors. Then Maria snarled, "She thought I really cut it. Damn, she thought I was for real." As the girls left the bathroom, Birdie opened her eyes and touched her hair as if to discover it for the first time. That night between whimpers and sighs, she told Cole in Elemeno about her experience with Maria, Cherise, and Cathy. As Birdie and Cole lay facing each other in the fetal position, Birdie expressed her disdain for the Nkrumah School. Cole admitted she rather liked it and her new girlfriends, so promised, "Don't worry, Bird. I'll make sure nobody messes with you."[39]

The next day Cole took Birdie back to the girls' bathroom after gym and confronted Maria and Cherise about the attempt to cut Birdie's hair. Cole's aggressive march and tone made Maria deny her actions. Cole grabbed Maria by her long thick hair . . . and whispered to her "Listen, metal mouth, Birdie isn't white. She's black. Just like me. So don't be messing with her again or I'll cut off all your hair for real."[40] As Maria pulled out of Cole's grip she commented, "So now I know."[41] After that event nobody ever messed with Birdie again.

Being accepted at Nkrumah School was arduous for Birdie. For a long time, no one even talked to her, but eventually she made her own friends. Cole contended with laughter and mocking at her ashy knees, totally oblivious to the African American custom

37. Ibid.
38. Ibid., 47.
39. Ibid., 48.
40. Ibid.
41. Ibid.

of cutting the ash with lotion. She asked her mother to buy Jergen's lotion so that they would avoid the ash and the ridicule from kids in gym class. Cole also became obsessive about her hair and grew frustrated to the point of tears and anger when her mother could not make cornrows like Keisha Taylor's in *Jet* magazine. Later that day Cole confided in Birdie that kids had laughed at her the previous week and called her "Miz Nappy." She lamented that none of the boys would come near her and that their mother didn't know about raising black kids. Cole added that they talked like white girls, according to an article about Black English in the *Ebony* magazine.[42] Though Cole was obviously concerned about expressing her blackness, their mother felt inadequate about helping her. Birdie consoled her mother's inadequacies while supporting Cole's need to be an acceptable black girl at the Nkrumah School. Birdie supported Cole's journey to embrace her black identity as a pre-teen and Cole legitimated Birdie as a black girl. Their mutual support, protection, and validation bears witness to their unconditional sisterly love.

Their love for each other was tested the most as they watched the demise of their parents' marriage. It all came to a head one July morning before they entered the Nkrumah School. The fighting escalated to shouting about Birdie's resemblance to a Sicilian. As Deck, their father, started the motor of his old Volvo packed with his clothes and books, he spoke in a slow soft tone:

> I know what my daughter looks like, thank you. Maybe you need to cut this naïve, color-blind posturing. In a country as racist as this, you're either black or you're white. And no daughter of mine is going to pass.[43]

As he drove off, little did Birdie know that his words foreshadowed her fate. Even though their parents separated over disagreements about many things, their mother conceded and allowed them to attend Nkrumah School, as their father had wanted.

42. Ibid., 53.
43. Ibid., 27.

During the weekends the girls would visit with their father. Birdie always felt when they were together that she became invisible to her father because he favored Cole. Occasionally, Birdie opted out of weekend visits with her father. One such weekend happened when a snow storm swept through Boston, making streets impassable and canceling school for a week.[44] Cole was in Roxbury and Birdie was home in the South End. Even though they talked daily, Cole seemed busy with school friends that lived in their dad's neighborhood and Cole could trudge to their houses to play. On Tuesday during that snow week, Cole told Birdie about their father's new girlfriend, Carmen. Cole thought she was beautiful. She fixed Cole's hair in a French twist, listened to music with her, and told her about sex. She admonished Birdie not to tell their mother about Carmen. However, at the end of the week when the rain began to wash the snow away and their father brought Cole home, Carmen was in the front passenger seat and Cole, waving halfheartedly, sat in the back seat. When Carmen greeted Birdie, she said she felt as if she already knew her because Cole had told her so much about her sister. Once in the privacy of their attic bedroom Cole spoke to Birdie in Elemeno about the fun she had had with Carmen the whole week, the card games they had played, and the books they had read aloud about Brazil, which they would all visit someday.[45] As Cole spoke, Birdie glimpsed a new life in Cole, "as if she had found some reflection of herself in this tall, cool woman."[46] Hearing about Cole's new adventures brought on a heavy grief for Birdie. During future weekend visits when Birdie would come along, Carmen would ignore Birdie and dote on Cole. As time progressed, Birdie recognized that everyone in her family was going their separate ways. Her mother was disappearing into the basement with her activist friends, her father into the writing of his book, Cole into her adolescence, and she into her Brown Sugars clique at Nkrumah.[47] Carmen superseded all she had

44. Ibid., 83.
45. Ibid., 91.
46. Ibid.
47. Ibid.

experienced from others who pointed out the differences between her and Cole—the textures of their hair, the tints of their skin, the shapes of their features. "But Carmen was the one to make [Birdie] feel that those things mattered . . . that differences were deeper than skin."[48] Carmen's behavior became so apparent that their father began to take notice.

On the other hand, Cole felt invisible and alone in the presence of Grandmother Lodge. One morning when the sisters were preparing for school, their mother announced they wouldn't attend school that day but would go to Cambridge to visit their grandmother. Cole was especially upset about missing school, and doing so to visit their grandmother, no less. The only time Grandmother Lodge ever acknowledged her was through the Christmas gift of a golliwog when she was very young, long before Nkrumah, where they learned what was wrong about dolls like Golliwog. His body was made of cloth and he had long limp arms and legs. His face was a perfect black circle with steel wool for hair shaped like a crescent. His huge white eyes were made of plastic with tiny black pupils, and his large red felt mouth revealed a disingenuous smile. Grandmother Lodge had given Sandy, their mother, a doll like Golli when she was a little girl. Cole loved Golli and slept with him every night even after becoming aware of why he was inappropriate for Nkrumah school children.

Grandmother Lodge always doted on Birdie, reminding her that she came from good stock as a descendent of Cotton Mather, while completely ignoring Cole. On this particular visit, Grandmother Lodge beckoned Birdie to her side using words of endearment, complimenting her on her appearance, and noting that she looked like Arabella, a distant cousin who lived in England. Even when Sandy pointed out the physical differences between Birdie and Arabella, grandmother commented that it was something in Birdie's face structure that resembled Arabella. While Birdie entertained Grandmother, Cole read a book that she had brought along. When Edna, a Caribbean woman, announced that the meal was ready, they gathered around the table to eat. Grandmother

48. Ibid.

continued her focus on Birdie, asking her questions about school. She had been instructed not to mention the name and nature of the Nkrumah School. However, in the midst of all the questions Birdie began to slip and their mother had to help out so that Grandmother would not discover the type of school they attended. As Birdie and Cole removed their plates from the table, they noticed their mother's posture seemed like a little girl as she asked her mother for money. As their grandmother wrote out the check, they could hear her disapproving whisper, "I don't know what you need this for, Sandra Lodge, but I hope you're not up to any funny business."[49] They left Grandmother's house before dessert. As they walked to the door, her grandmother looked down at Birdie, who began to feel small and pitiful, and said, "You know, Birdie, you could be Italian. Or even French. Couldn't she, Sandy?"[50] Unexpectedly their mother didn't retort or debate but with a sad smile said, "Yes, Mother, she could be."[51] Her mother took her hand and they walked swiftly to the car where Cole was already waiting in the front seat.

By springtime Birdie had become good at the jump rope game, double Dutch. One day, while jumping to the rhythmic chants of her girlfriends, Redbone—one of her mother's friends and father's enemies—called to her from behind a fence adjacent to the playground and asked about her father and mother's whereabouts. When she insisted she needed to leave, pointing out Cole in the distance, Redbone said, "Yeah, I see her. What happened there? You sure you got the same daddy?" Then Redbone asked again, "Tell me, how's your daddy doing? I haven't see him in ages either. He don't got time for the revolution."[52] Although appearing to sound casual, she was beginning to panic and started to run away. Remembering what her father had coached her to say in such circumstances, she responded, "No, he's writing a masterpiece. He

---

49. Ibid., 106–7.
50. Ibid., 107.
51. Ibid.
52. Ibid., 109.

doesn't have time for you."[53] As she moved toward the school officials, Redbone said he would miss her. That statement sounded strange. As soon as she turned and said, "I'm not going anywhere,"[54] he snapped her picture with an automatic camera.

After school while her mother drove her and Birdie home, she told them about Redbone. Her mother became unnerved and almost hit an oncoming car. She quickly pulled into the parking lot of a fast food restaurant and grabbed Birdie's arm and asked her to tell her again what had happened. Birdie, frightened and nervous, listened to the urgency of her mother's voice as she said, "If he ever comes near you again, scream your little head off till someone comes to the rescue. Hear me?"[55] Cole was admonished to keep watch over Birdie.

When the weekend came, their father Deck came by to pick them up for a visit to the museum. Uncharacteristically, this time he focused on Birdie to come back with him. While Cole entered the car and sat in the back seat with Carmen, their father tried and tried to get Birdie to come along. She felt the reason for his new attention to her was because he had finally realized that Carmen would not speak to her. Yet, Birdie opted not to go. As Birdie stood in front of her bedroom window in a daze of dreams about only her and her father traveling to Egypt, her mother came bounding up the steps and into the doorway. It was obvious that her mom had been crying after an intense conversation with her friend Jane about being traced, being paranoid, and someone finding out about something.[56] She wanted to treat Birdie to a banana split at the ice cream parlor. While there, her mother cursed about Deck moving to Brazil to write his book. She felt it was an excuse and referred to him as an "escapist overintellectualized creep."[57] Their conversation moved to Birdie's opinion of Carmen. "She's a bitch,"

53. Ibid.
54. Ibid., 110.
55. Ibid., 111.
56. Ibid., 113.
57. Ibid., 114.

Birdie stated using a word she had never used before. Her mother responded:

> So, Miss Black and Beautiful doesn't think you're good enough, huh? You probably remind her of me, and that's what they're all trying to forget these days, you know—that they ever dabbled in the nitty-gritty land of miscegenation. Well, you can tell her and that righteous brotherman—your father—that it's my white ass that's going to end up in prison![58]

With that statement they left the ice cream parlor. Birdie's mother's nervous energy filled the car on the ride home.

A few days later Birdie and Cole's father took them to their favorite restaurant, a Polynesian place that only the girls and their father frequented. However, on this occasion their mother joined them. The girls ordered their favorite foods and drinks. During the meal their mother tried to convince their father that the four of them should reunite and move to Canada immediately. But Deck responded that now he had other persons to think about. Their mom's fit of rage brought loud cursing, unsettling Birdie enough to spill her drink. The accidental spill froze everyone. Cole comforted her sister and asked her not to cry. The awkward moment resulted in the girls going to the bathroom for a long reprieve, Birdie speaking Elemeno to herself in the mirror, and Cole silently sitting in one of the stalls. When they emerged, the girls and their parents left the restaurant for the brownstone on Columbus Avenue. When they arrived, their mother said Cole would be spending the night with her father. Birdie protested that it was a school night but her mother's quick response silenced her. Birdie's father suddenly pulled her close and hugged her so tightly, it hurt. After pulling away to get some air he explained that Boston, America was in bad shape and it was going to get worse. "Black people need to start thinking internationally."[59] He then announced that he, Cole, and Carmen were going to Brazil, for a short stay. Cole's eyes met Birdie's and she attempted a smile. She said, "Tell Mum I love

58. Ibid.
59. Ibid., 121.

67

her, okay? Tell her I'll talk to her later?"[60] Their father's face held
a look of abandonment as he turned, cleared his throat, shuffled
newspapers on the front seat, and started the engine. Birdie and
her beloved sister, Cole, did not say goodbye. Cole got into the
back seat and waved at Birdie as the Volvo eased away from the
curb. Cole pressed her face against the window as they held each
other's gaze. Seeking solace and answers, Birdie bounded up the
stairs to her mother's room only to find her seated on the floor
crying. Only later that afternoon when her mother started to move
about the kitchen to prepare lunch did Birdie feel safe enough to
ask why her father and sister were going to Brazil. Sandy said she
would explain later.

During the night while Birdie lay in bed half asleep, she heard
voices in the house. Someone came into her room in the attic with
a shadow behind her. She could sense from the breathing pattern
that it was Cole. She opened her eyes just enough to verify it was
her. Cole brushed a hair from Birdie's face. With a sad smile she
stroked Birdie's hair back and spoke in Elemeno. Then Cole, wearing a head wrap and African garments much like Carmen, tucked
something under the covers next to Birdie. Out of the corner of
her eye Birdie could see it was Golliwog. Cole never let anyone
touch Golliwog. Birdie wanted to rise and hug her sister but could
not move.[61] Cole and the figure that stood behind her left the dark
room.

Later that night, about 5:00 AM, Birdie's mother pulled off
her blankets to wake her up. She was almost unrecognizable with
penny-colored hair in two braids, red lipstick, and red scratches
on her cheeks.[62] Her mother told her to get dressed while she
randomly put items in a duffle bag for travel. She mumbled inco-
herently words that included felony, the fuzz, and prison time.[63]
Birdie asked about Cole and Papa. Sandy told her they had gone
to Brazil. She confirmed that Cole and her father had been in the

60. Ibid.
61. Ibid., 123.
62. Ibid.
63. Ibid., 124.

house that night and that they had left Birdie a package from Deck, admonishing her not to open it until they were on the road. Just as her mother was pulling her toward the bedroom door, Birdie pulled back the bed covers and found Golliwog and put him in her duffle bag with her other belongings. Birdie and Sandy packed their meager belongings into their green Pinto and drove off.

The daylight assured Birdie and Sandy that Boston was miles behind them. Birdie asked her mother why they were running, why Cole and Papa had gone to Brazil, and when the decision had been made. In between long periods of silence, miles of traveling, and one motel room after another, Sandy explained that the FBI was after them. The Cointelpro or Counter Intelligence Program, an arm of the FBI with its secret and illegal methods, sought to discredit and incarcerate political activists like Angela Davis and members of the Black Panther Party. They were on the lam avoiding capture by the FBI's Cointelpro.[64]

Day after day they slept in motels in cities all along the eastern United States, living off the money Grandmother Lodge had given them. One morning early in their refugee life, Birdie found herself sitting across the table from her mother at a diner in Maine. Birdie didn't know the reason why her family had split up and her father and Cole had gone to Brazil with Carmen in tow. The box Deck and Cole had left for Birdie had the word "Negrobilia" written on the side.

> It included a Black Nativity program from the Nkrumah School, a fisted pick (the smell of someone's scalp oil still lingering in between the sharp black teeth), a black Barbie doll head, an informational tourist pamphlet on Brazil, the silver Egyptian necklace inscribed with hieroglyphics that [Deck] had bought [Birdie] at a museum . . . years before, and a James Brown eight-track cassette with a faded sticker in the corner that said "Nubian Notion," the name of the record shop on Washington Street.[65]

64. Ibid., 126–27.
65. Ibid., 127.

The Negrobilia box and Golliwog was all Birdie had left of her papa and her beloved Cole. While her mother spoke very little after leaving Boston, the morning in the Maine diner was different. Her mother said that the FBI would be looking for a white woman with a black child. It was a fact that Birdie could pass, her mother explained, with her "straight hair, pale skin, and general phenotypic resemblance to the Caucasoid race,"[66] and that this would likely throw off the FBI. Birdie's body was the solution to her mother's need to be incognito. Excited about her brilliant idea, Sandy asked Birdie what new name she wanted. Before Birdie could answer, she suggested the name Jesse because it was the name of Sandy's great-grandmother who was a suffragette. She suggested Birdie come up with a last name saying, "You've got a lot of choices, babe. You can be anything. Puerto Rican, Sicilian, Pakistani, Greek, . . . anything really."[67] Her mother then proceeded to concoct a story that Birdie's full name would be Jesse Goldman, the daughter of the deceased David Goldman, a Jewish professor of classics, just like her real papa. Sandy took the name Sheila.

For four years Sandy and Birdie ran from what her mother thought would be capture and imprisonment in a Federal prison, staying in motels and communes.[68] That Redbone had approached Birdie on the playground at Nkrumah School was evidence for Sandy that he worked for the FBI and wanted to know information about her parents. That incident helped Sandy conclude they had to run. And so they ran, staying only for short periods in various places in upstate New York, Maine, and Pennsylvania with Birdie passing as a Jewish girl named Jesse Goldman.

Not a day went by that Birdie did not think about how and when she would reunite with Cole and her papa. Birdie remembered good times when her family was together, especially times with Cole in their attic bedroom playing make believe and speaking Elemeno. Birdie was determined to reunite with Cole. Nothing and no one would stop her quest to find her sister. She persistently

66. Ibid., 128.

67. Ibid., 130–31.

68. Ibid., 135.

asked her mother why the family split up but her mother would not respond. Birdie was the embodiment of fortitude—resolute in mind, spirit, and body to find her beloved sister Cole and her father. To keep her memories alive, Birdie rehearsed Elemeno and examined each item in her Negrobilia box and Golliwog.

In the fourth year of their fugitive existence Sandy decided to settle into a home in the country. Therefore she chose a little country town in New Hampshire that was just adjacent to a university town where she could get a job.[69] They rented a two-bedroom wood frame house complete with a barn and horses on Bridgewater Road owned by a professor and his wife, who lived about a mile or so adjacent to the property.[70] Sandy convinced Walter Marsh to rent her the property and gained a lead for a research assistant's job at his university, all with a thin, dark-complexioned adolescent sitting by her side.[71] For the next four and a half years Sandy supported them with her research assistant's job and tutoring special needs kids in the little town. Throughout this time she existed and even thrived as Shelia, the Jewish widow. She started a relationship with a white man named Jim, and over time talked less and less about the Feds searching for them. Her relationship with Jim grew to a level of unconditional trust and she eventually revealed their true identity to him.

All the while Sandy reminded Birdie to continue passing as Jesse Goldman, and Birdie complied with her life of passing as a Jewish white girl because she loved her mother. Yet she found tacit ways to resist her clandestine identity. On occasion she convinced herself that passing was research that would help her papa with his book and she would report the data during their time of reunion.[72] She would review each item in her Negrobilia box regularly, perhaps to keep the memories of her father and sister fresh and to maintain her loyalty to them. She played games that helped her remember even the most trivial details about Nkrumah School, the

69. Ibid., 143.
70. Ibid., 144.
71. Ibid., 150.
72. Ibid., 189.

family home, her father's apartment, Elemeno words, and smells, sounds, and images that brought her hope that she would one day reunite with her father and sister.[73] Even her mother's decision to stop home schooling her and to allow her to enter eighth grade at a local school did not deter her resolve to find her sister and father. As her mother's relationship deepened with Jim, Birdie resisted any resemblance of a daughter/father relationship with him. However, she did form relationships with a few girls and boys at school. She maintained the clandestine identity of Jesse or Jessica, the white Jewish girl, whose best friend in the New Hampshire school was Mona, a white girl who lived in a trailer park. They talked about boys and sex as a common point of their relationship. Birdie was surprised to discover there was another biracial girl in the eighth grade, who was visibly black. A white couple had adopted Samantha Taper.

For three years her determination to maintain her identity as a black girl named Birdie at home and the Jewish girl named Jessica at school continued without her schoolmates knowing the truth. Then one day her life as Jessica came to a screeching halt at a house party. The host's only bathroom had a long waiting line so she went outside to relieve herself. As she walked into the thicket behind the house she ran into Samantha who was also relieving herself outside. As both Samantha and Birdie finished and started walking back to the house, she asked Samantha, "What color do you think I am?"[74] Samantha didn't answer but smiled and then walked toward the house. Then Birdie asked her "What color are you?" and Samantha replied, "I'm black, like you."[75] Then Samantha asked if she was coming back inside but Birdie only looked at the ground. As the drizzling became a steady downpour she found herself walking toward home down the wet asphalt. When she arrived home drenched she crept upstairs to her mother's bedroom. Longing for her mother to comfort her with stories of life with Cole and papa before going on the lam, instead she found her mom and

73. Ibid., 190.
74. Ibid., 285.
75. Ibid., 286.

Jim sleeping and turned toward her own bedroom. Birdie packed her box of Negrobilia, underwear, a photograph of her and her mom when they first arrived in New Hampshire, and for some unknown reason, the Star of David. She silently went downstairs and searched through the emergency drawer for all the money she could find, then headed to town.[76] As she passed the silver, clear lake on Bridgeman Road she wondered if she would "forever be fleeing in the dark, abandoning parts of myself that I no longer wanted, in search of some part that had escaped [her]. Killing one girl in order to let the other one free."[77] In the dawn of a new day Birdie boarded a bus for Boston.

Birdie Lee arrived in Boston on a cold wet day with only forty-five dollars and a determination to find her Aunt Dorothy (Dot) Lee. Her only hope to find Aunt Dot was an address on a postcard she had found in her mother's book. She didn't know when or how the postcard had reached her mother.[78] With the help of a homeless black woman, she found her brownstone at Forty-six Montgomery Street in the South End.[79] After knocking on the door, she was once again united with her Aunt Dot and now a new first cousin, a little girl named Taj. Her Aunt Dot fed her and invited her to stay as long as she wanted, but encouraged Birdie Lee to call her mother to let her know she was okay. Several days later Birdie woke to the sound of her Aunt Dot talking on the phone. Birdie heard the words, "Yes, Sandy,"[80] and almost immediately saw her aunt's small frame coming toward her. Dot had called her mother using Birdie's school ID to locate Jessica Goldman's mother in New Hampshire. Birdie took the phone from her aunt with an expression of dismay on her face. Her words, "Hi, Mum,"[81] were met with expletives and shouting. Sandy concluded her comments with "Give me Dot."[82]

76. Ibid., 287–88.
77. Ibid., 289.
78. Ibid., 294.
79. Ibid., 295.
80. Ibid., 317.
81. Ibid., 318.
82. Ibid., 319.

In the days that followed Birdie's conversation with her mother, she wandered the streets of Boston, trying to reacquaint herself with the city. Her Aunt Dot, a teacher, went to work each day and little Taj went to school. One evening when Dot came home and found Birdie listening to music and sorting through the contents of her box of Negrobilia spread before her, Dot suggested that Birdie go out for some fresh air.[83] When Birdie returned, she found Sandy and Jim sitting with Dot. After Jim and Dot left the kitchen so that Birdie and Sandy could talk, her mother told her she must leave with them and return to New Hampshire. Their conversation about staying safe from the Feds ended with Sandy calling Birdie Jess and telling her she must pack her things so they could all return to New Hampshire. Birdie Lee reminded her mother of her real name. As Sandy reached for Birdie, she ducked and ran out the door into the dark street. Mother and daughter wrestled in the street with Sandy swearing loudly until lights came on in nearby apartments. Neighbors' silhouettes appeared in the windows. Finally, Sandy slapped Birdie across her face and caught her in a headlock. Dot and Jim ran into the street pleading with Sandy that there was another way to resolve the problem when two police officers drove up. Sandy softened her grip and Birdie broke free. When the police asked her about their relationship, she said Sandy was a family friend and that she lived with her Aunt Dot. While the police looked skeptically back and forth between Birdie and Dot, they admonished them to keep the noise down or they would come back. When the cops were gone, Sandy told Birdie to get into the car but she refused. Dot promised Sandy she would take good care of Birdie, that she would come around if given some time. With that promise her mother drove away with Jim.[84]

Birdie Lee defied her mother and six years of passing as a Jewish white girl. This was her ultimate act of fortitude, an unwavering determination to stay the course of claiming her black-white mixed-race identity and reuniting with the black members of her family. Up until this point she had respected her mother's wishes

83. Ibid., 330.
84. Ibid., 332–36.

to pass as a white girl in public while holding onto her African heritage in private. She refused to live the lie of being white.

After Birdie and her mother's altercation in the street, she went about reconnecting with classmates who might help her locate her father and sister. She discovered that Deck and Cole Lee had stayed only two years in Brazil before moving back to the United States. His old friend, Ronnie, told her he had bumped into her father in San Francisco coming out of a library on Mission Street with a pile of books.[85] Ronnie recalled that Deck had given him his address in Oakland, California, and passed the address on to Birdie.

With the address of where her father had lived just two years earlier, Birdie turned her energies to finding money to travel to San Francisco. She recalled how Sandy Lee would get money from her mother, so she went to visit her grandmother, while promising her Aunt Dot she would return the same day. However, Birdie found it necessary to ingratiate herself to her grandmother to get money and that took an overnight stay. In fact, in exchange for money Birdie promised her grandmother Sandy's address, but wrote down a Woodstock address, a place she and Sandy had driven through once. With money in hand, Birdie convinced her grandmother that she must leave for San Francisco that very day, even if she had to fly standby. Doris the housekeeper called a Boston Coach for Birdie and she left for the airport.[86]

Birdie purchased a ticket for US Air flight 237. She called her Aunt Dot to apologize for not coming back to their apartment as she had promised. After landing in San Francisco, Birdie took a taxi to the Oakland apartment address that Ronnie had given her in hopes that she would be reunited with her father. No one answered the phone and on arrival no one answered the door. Pondering her next choices, to return to Boston or find a place to stay for the night, Birdie decided to go around to the back of the apartment. There she saw a dog on the couch and a television running as she peered into the window on tiptoes. She found another

85. Ibid., 353–55.
86. Ibid., 372–74.

window cracked open and she crawled into the apartment.[87] While in the apartment she nervously examined the space for evidence that it belonged to her father. There were no photographs or clear evidence that the apartment was her father's. Her hands shook as she examined a book about Liberia that was on the night stand. The dog followed her from room to room but turned toward the front door at the sound of approaching heavy footsteps. The door opened and she heard a familiar man's voice chastising the dog, Spanky, for pissing on the floor.[88] When the man approached the kitchen and saw Birdie holding a coffee pot, his cursing words stopped mid-sentence. In silence they stared at each other until Birdie said, "It's me."[89] Deck Lee's silence seemed to last longer until he whispered, "I told her you'd show up sooner or later. I told her."[90] He welcomed Birdie, although with a slightly sad smile. Over instant coffee while waiting for the frozen macaroni and cheese to cook, Deck talked to his daughter. Birdie first inquired about Cole and he responded that she was attending college at Berkeley. He verified that he had been back in the country from Brazil for five years yet had not contacted his sister Dot or anyone else. Their conversation meandered through excuses for not looking for her over the past five years, reasons for not taking her to Brazil, theories on racism and mulatto existence in the United States, and the publication of his book after years of research and writing. Birdie sat through it all anxiously waiting to hear her father say he would take her to see Cole.[91] They ate in silence and then he insisted on driving her to see Cole instead of allowing her to find her own way, as Birdie was determined to do that night. When they arrived at the wood-frame house where Cole lived with her college roommates, Deck invited her back to his apartment to stay if she wished, but Birdie said no. He asked if he would see her

87. Ibid., 383–84.
88. Ibid., 386.
89. Ibid., 387.
90. Ibid.
91. Ibid., 387–94.

again and even though she wanted to punish him for being a bad father, she said yes.[92]

Upon knocking at the door, Birdie discovered that Cole was not home. From her Latina housemate she received directions to the coffee shop where Cole was studying for an exam. She walked to the coffee shop in the cold rain, her grandfather's cashmere coat now soaking wet and her hair hanging in wet clumps.[93] Upon entering the coffee shop Birdie paused in the doorway to survey the crowded room. Her eyes fell on a young woman sitting in the back of the café who she was sure was Cole. Her stare seemed to erase all other people in the shop. The young woman looked up as if someone had called her name, then looked back at the woman talking to her at their table. But she looked up again and her eyes met Birdie's. They held one another's gaze for at least a full minute. Then Birdie found herself floating toward Cole. They embraced each other tightly for a long time, neither saying a word nor shedding a tear, only allowing the sounds of the café to validate the reality of their reunion.[94] Cole's friend asked whether Birdie was the one in the photograph and Cole nodded, while clutching Birdie's hand. "This is her," she said in a quiet, throaty voice. "I'm going home with her now. We've got some catching up to do."[95] With those words, the sisters began their life anew.

This coming-of-age story of race and identity of two black/white mixed-race sisters demonstrates the fortitude of the mulatta, primarily amid her familial relationships, and to a lesser extent among her peer relationships. Birdie's fortitude took the form of volition and strength of mind to press persistently toward the reunion with her black father and biracial sister. Such fortitude does not falter when faced with death-dealing obstacles, but perseveres with courage to accomplish its goals. Just as Sandra Lange in chapter 1 demonstrated fortitude to reunite with her mother, so too did Ruby Doris Smith and Diane Nash embody fortitude as young

92. Ibid., 399.
93. Ibid., 400.
94. Ibid., 402.
95. Ibid., 403.

female activists in SNCC during the civil rights movement of the 1960s and 1970s.

Fortitude is not exclusively a character trait or practice of racial/ethnic minoritized women and girls. However, fortitude takes unique shape among women and girls of African ancestry when it is prompted by struggles caused by the intersecting injustices of race, class, gender, and sexuality. Certainly women of other ethnicities can also show fortitude. Yet, a black/white mixed-race woman or girl who is aware of her African heritage and the imposition of the problem of color in a country rooted in a history of enslaving African-descended people has special reasons for fortitude. Fortitude seeks to challenge and dismantle racist practices born of white supremacist ideologies. Birdie's fortitudinous actions of remembering the minute details about her father and sister, resisting passing as white in the privacy of her home, and tangibly remembering her African heritage through the box of Negrobilia are all forms of resistance to white supremacy.

Fortitude is essential for a liberating hope at the intersection of race, gender, class, and sexual orientation. Strength of mind and volition are vital components of African-descended women and girls who seek to transform systemic practices rooted in racism, sexism, classism, and heterosexism. An *emancipatory* hope demands embodied fortitude like that of Mrs. Lula Elizabeth Cooper, the mother of Alvin Alley, who like legions of black women have been raped and/or trafficked because of their female genitalia and the color of their skin. Enfleshed fortitude is evident in black women who daily endure assaults on their character simply because they are female, black, and poor. Fortitude is incarnated in lesbian women who exist at the intersection of being female, black, poor, and same-gender loving. As indicated at the outset of this chapter, fortitude is intellectual and spiritual strength to persevere amid impossible conditions. Hope that expects a society governed by God's liberating justice for all humankind, regardless of one's social location, requires intellectual and spiritual strength.

The African-descended woman or girl who understands her attribute of fortitude as a gift from God, to use for God's purposes of justice, peace, and love, possesses an enhanced sense of self-awareness that is Christian at its core. Emancipatory hope—a liberating expectation that God will act in favor of those cast down and destroyed because of white supremacist patriarchal heterosexist practices—requires a Christian spirituality that incarnates fortitude along with forgiveness and femaleship. Such *emancipatory hope*, however, is incomplete without freedom, the subject of the next chapter.

4

Freedom

FREEDOM IS AN ONTOLOGICAL ideal, a way of being in the world that defies the hard spiritual, physical, and psychological realities that so commonly enervate the minds and bodies of young African American women. Freedom is the capacity of an individual to focus on what is hoped for, such as material freedom, while negotiating daunting circumstances of struggle and strife, such as human enslavement or economic oppression. It is a mind-set that holds onto dignity and integrity when powers of domination seek to rob or destroy one of dignity and integrity. Freedom is a state of mind that governs the actions of the body even when abused, battered, and ultimately destroyed. Practices of material freedom, such as the gritty strength of a person who rejects psychological incarceration while her body is behind bars in state or federal prison, is freedom. Practices of freedom and beliefs in freedom enhance one another.

An individual cannot experience freedom without a sense of self.[1] A sense of self clarifies questions of "Who am I?" and "What do I want to do?"[2] Having a sense of self helps an individual make clear decisions, take responsibility for their actions, and restore their dignity when it is compromised. Freedom, as a component

1. Thurman, *Deep is the Hunger*, 62–142.
2. Ibid., 63.

of the sense of self, decides whether to go around opposition or "knock all opposition out of the way."[3] Freedom is being centered in knowing who one is as one decides on a course of action in the face of opposition. Freedom, rooted in a sense of self, never submits "one's inner togetherness, one's sense of inner authority"[4] to those who seek to destroy the self. Freedom derived from a sense of self recalibrates imbalances caused by overt or covert verbal attacks on one's personhood. For a Christian, essential to this sense of self is acknowledgement of and dependence on God who is the divine source of an individual's sense of self. The one who acknowledges their need for God's composure amid frantic situations, God's eyes to see love amid the world's ugliness, God's grace and patience amid interpersonal conflict, and God's comfort and rest at the end of a hard day's work,[5] truly has a sense of self that exhibits freedom. Finally, because "[t]he central emphasis of the teaching of Jesus centers upon the relationship of individual to individual, and of all individuals to God,"[6] a sense of self must affirm the relational aspects of all that it takes to make the individual have a sense of self, including those aspects related to freedom.

This freedom as an entity of a sense of self is freedom of the individual. However, freedom is also social/communal. When a group of oppressed people is unified in their understanding of freedom, they become a social force for material liberation. For African Americans, the ideal of freedom was nurtured in the will and deepest desires of the enslaved human being and resulted in strategies of material freedom. Strong-willed people experience communal freedom when they resolve to stay the course, to focus on things hoped for and imagined by the collective or community. Evidence of unrelenting determination never to accept the material reality of African enslavement is found in memoirs and the Negro spirituals. When enslaved African descendants sang, "Oh freedom, oh freedom, oh freedom over me. And before I'd

3. Ibid., 66.
4. Ibid., 80.
5. Ibid., 104.
6. Ibid., 108.

be a slave I'll be buried in my grave and go home to my Lord and be free,"[7] they invoked words of resistance to enslavement in the midst of physical and material bondage. By this song they forthrightly rejected otherworldly expectations of freedom—that freedom would come only in heaven—and declared aggressive means to obtain material freedom for themselves now even if it brought death to the enslaved African. This indeed happened. Frankie and Doug Quimby told Marian E. Barnes the story of the Ibo Landing, published in *Talk that Talk: An Anthology of African-American Storytelling.* When slave traders went to the Ibo tribe in Nigeria, West Africa they convinced eighteen men to come with them to America supposedly to work for fair wages. After the group of Ibo people arrived at St. Simon's Island, Georgia they discovered that they had been tricked and were to be sold into slavery. All eighteen men decided that they would rather be dead than enslaved. Chained together, they prayed and declared that water brought them and water would take them away. Then they walked backwards together into Dunbar Creek and drowned themselves. As they were going down they sang a song in their Ibo language that continues to be sung today in English as "Oh Freedom." Today Dunbar Creek on St. Simon's Island is a popular tourist attraction to which people are drawn because of the courageous story of the eighteen Ibo youth. Some visitors to Dunbar Creek on certain moonlit nights tell of hearing voices wailing and chains clinking.[8] The song of these eighteen people who defied enslavement unto death has inspired insurrection and resistance of African-descended groups throughout history. It was sung during the post-slavery era and during the civil rights movement and continues today as a musical declaration of resistance to oppression.

Communal freedom was also evident in the efforts of protestors during the civil rights movement of the 1960s and 1970s. Whether as a community on the picket lines, in protest marches, or in mass meetings in churches and synagogues, civil rights activists gathered in community and physically demonstrated their

7. Jones, *Wade in the Water.*
8. Barnes and Goss, eds., *Talk That Talk*, 139.

common ideological belief in freedom. In addition to the Negro spiritual, "Oh Freedom," the community would sing and often redact other Negro spirituals such as "Ain't gonna let nobody turn me round . . . Marching up to Freedom's way." The spiritual "We Shall Overcome Someday," was and continues to be a frequent lyrical statement of the ideal of freedom for oppressed people. The lyrics were as fluid and unique as the community or individual (i.e., entertainer) that sang them. This verse, which speaks of freedom, is an example of such fluidity:

> The truth shall make us free, the truth shall make us free;
> The truth shall make us free someday.
> Oh, deep in my heart, I do believe,
> The truth shall make us free someday.[9]

When the community of civil rights activists sang the above verse, they declared that the truth about racial and economic injustice would lead to freedom for all the oppressed. Martin Luther King, Jr. believed that freedom for the oppressed also meant freedom for the oppressors. The stanza is a fitting example of something hoped for; the community hopes that someday they will be free, which leads to a correlation between freedom and *emancipatory* hope.

Freedom as the core ideal and motivation for life of the individual and the community is inextricably tied to a Christian hope that is liberating. Freedom connotes liberation. While it is defined here as an ontological ideal, a way of being in the world that defies oppression, it also connotes an infinite aspiration of the individual and her community to be materially free of oppression. God, as the Holy Spirit, moves through the politics and practices of women and men who genuinely believe in the end of racial and economic oppression, as well as, occasionally, through those who do not seek to end oppression. The Holy Spirit works within the individual and her community, who embody freedom, to bring about the expectation of material freedom for all humankind.

9. "We Shall Overcome," http://www.lyricsfreak.com/v/various+artists/we+shall+overcome_10170009.html.

Thus freedom is about striving for the ultimate spiritual self and the community to thrive in an ontological ideal that defies spiritual, physical, and psychological oppression of the mind and body. Within the tragic relationships of the mulatta, we find clues to what true freedom means. This chapter examines individual freedom through the lives of same-gender–loving young women who are black/white mixed-race and African American using a biographical documentary about English boxer Michele Aboro and interview materials about Dee Rees, screenwriter and director of the award-winning film *Pariah*. For both Michele and Dee, freedom means claiming an identity that is your own true self. In turn, such individual freedom shapes communal freedom that practices prophetic activities on behalf of same-gender–loving young women buoyed by an *emancipatory* hope. With a focus primarily on the black/white biracial lesbian, this chapter seeks answers to questions that include: What is true freedom when you are biracial in a racist society? And what is its nature? At what price is freedom? How does freedom bring emancipatory hope?

Michele Aboro, English Championship Boxer

What does freedom look like for Michele Aboro, a black/white mixed-race lesbian who grew up in England's south London? The intersection of gender, race, sexuality, and class converge in the body of Michele Aboro and threaten her true freedom. Yet Michele responds to this challenge in several ways that include professional boxing. The documentary film *A Knock Out* by Tessa Boerman and Samuel Reiziger[10] is the text that places Michele Aboro at the center of discourse about freedom, a text that illustrates the intersection of gender, ethnicity, class, and sexuality and the complexities surrounding mulatta existence.

When the documentary *A Knock Out* was released in 2004, Michele Aboro was thirty-seven years old, just on the upper limits of what is now considered as young adulthood in North America.

---

10. Boerman and Reiziger, *A Knock Out*.

Born on July 17, 1967 in London, England, her father is an African-descended Nigerian and her mother white. The biographical film opens with Michele walking toward a public housing apartment in a working-class neighborhood where her mother, Stella, lives. The camera follows Michele as she describes her old neighborhood and captures her unscripted confrontation with two teenage boys driving recklessly on the streets amid children playing, some of whom are her relatives. Though the teenage boys threaten her with expletives, Michele does not back off and neither does she return similar language. She appears ready for a physical altercation if necessary. The teens speed away and she continues her narration of what it was like growing up in the neighborhood. Michele's lean and buff body is clothed in jeans, a plain shirt, and a leather jacket. Her almost clean-shaven head leaves one guessing whether she is male or female. Subsequently her mother, Stella, tells the biographers of the long history of Michele's dress that was gender ambiguous for those who didn't know her. Stella recalled that when Michele was very young, she would fix Michele's long hair in one or two braids and send her off to school in a dress. However, Michele would pack jeans and a T-shirt in her backpack and would change into them on the way to school and wear them back home in the evening. Ponytails and little dresses were never Michele's choice of hairstyle and dress, recalled Stella. Her mother suggests that as early as primary school Michele resisted traditional dress codes that defined gender, femininity, and sexuality.

As a teen, Stella recounted, Michele was skinny and wore a huge afro. Stella and Louise, Michele's younger sister, recalled Michele being arrested by the police on several occasions because they thought she was a black male. On one occasion Stella remembered Michele being picked up and badly beaten by the police. On another occasion the police picked Michele off the street and detained her in jail for two days without allowing her to contact her mother. Stella was frantic with worry, not knowing where Michele was. Stella believed that Michele's appearance as a black male fueled the racial profiling by police. Nonetheless, Michele resolved to dress as she chose, but this escalated her stress and struggle to come of age in a racist and homophobic society.

The racism that Michele and her family experienced was more than racial profiling by London's police. When the family lived in Shepherd's Bush, Stella recollected that someone threw a gas boom into the basement of their apartment simply because Stella had a mixed-race child. Michele stated, "Black kids didn't like us and white kids didn't like us. You always felt you had to come up to their game to be accepted. You were pushed past your limits to be accepted."[11] Michele learned to focus all her anger into kickboxing and other sports at a youth club that she joined.

Michele found good childhood friends in Andre and Julian, two black males, at the youth club. They spoke about her unbridled anger at those who sought to hurt her because she was black to some and biracial to others as well as a non-stereotypical female. Boxing channeled her anger. Andre and Julian talked of their un-conditional acceptance of Michele even though she was coming out as a lesbian before their eyes. They were amazed at and sup-portive of her athletic skills. It was with the support of Andre and Julian that Michele began to develop her skills as a boxer.

Despite economic, racial, gender, and sexual struggles in Lon-don, Michele Aboro rose to fame, becoming a three-time winner of the WIBF World Champion Junior Featherweight boxing title. According to her biographers in the documentary, some recog-nized her as being, pound for pound, the best fighter in the world. Michele fought twenty-one fights with twenty-one wins, eighteen of which were knockouts.[12] As a professional boxer she struggled with the increased commercialization of women's sports. Her fame as a boxer took a turn for the worse when boxing authorities deemed her as being "[un]promotable,"[13] unmarketable. Boxing promoters in Amsterdam and Germany wanted to force Michele to present more feminine and less "hard" images of herself. Pro-moters critiqued her for fighting too much like a man. Only once

11. Ibid.
12. Ibid.
13. Ibid.

did Michele submit to the pressure of the promoters and allowed them to dye her short afro platinum blonde, put makeup on her face, and adorn her in a black sequined gown. Referring to the photo that promoters took on this occasion, her mother Stella said that was not her Michele. "It's a beautiful picture of a beautiful girl" but it was not her Michele. Promoters also wanted Michele to pose naked in magazines.[14] Michele responded that she could not hide her true identity and vowed never to give up her freedom to be her own unique self again. Her refusal to "vamp" up her image cost Michele her boxing career. The boxing industry abandoned her. At the time of the making of the documentary Michele was working as a stagehand with a music production company. Before the documentary ends by fading to black, with head bowed, Michele says, "When it comes to boxing I could make a lot of money, but who am I?"

What is freedom for a black/white mixed-race lesbian woman? At what price is her freedom? Michele Aboro answers these questions through her decision to be free to choose an authentic identity consistent with her gender, race/ethnicity, and sexual orientation. Freedom for Michele means sacrificing professional boxing that she loves because the powers that govern that profession want to force her to be inauthentic. The sacrifice is economically and emotionally painful. The sacrifice of her vocation as a professional boxer is also spiritually debilitating because she can no longer be a female athlete who enjoys her sport and models the same for younger female athletes. The spirit of women or men thrives when they live into their calling. And that is what Michele longs to do. Yet, her resolve to be free from the commercialization of professional female boxing shows a sense of self that does not compromise her identity with all its intersecting complexities of gender, race, class, and sexual orientation.

14. Ibid.

Dee Rees, Screenwriter and Film Director

The documentary on the life of Michele Aboro is juxtaposed with the life of screenwriter and film director Dee Rees, who is an out lesbian African American young adult. Rees garnered the attention of the entertainment industry and moviegoers with the release of her commercial film *Pariah*, a coming-of-age story about an African American teenage girl, Alike, who seeks to discover her authentic self amid her sexual attraction to girls. Rees wrote the script for *Pariah* and used the first act as her thesis project to graduate from New York University's graduate film program.[15] Rees exercised her freedom to live fully into her love for writing after a less fulfilling career in marketing. During an interview with *Lesbian News* she is quoted as saying, "Screenwriting is a way of actually seeing your writing come to life, your work done, so I quit my job and went to film school."[16] In another interview with *The Crisis* magazine, Rees said, "I really wanted to tell stories that were socially conscious, interesting and stories that just let people view themselves and the world around them in a more meaningful way."[17] Even a master's degree in business administration did not convince the then twenty-seven-year-old Nashville, Tennessee native to stay in the corporate world.

Dee Rees wrote the script for *Pariah* while navigating her own "coming out" process.[18] Seventeen-year-old Alike, the protagonist, straddles two worlds: that of her traditional family and that of her secret life as a lesbian, while grappling with her sexual identity and the need to belong at home and among friends.[19] Rees indicated that the movie "is semiautobiographical as she also struggled with her own identity as a lesbian and coming out to her family."[20] She acknowledged her own emotional struggle when coming out to

---

15. Joiner, "Visible Lives," 30-34.
16. John, "I am Your Sister," 22–25.
17. Joiner, "Visible Lives," 30.
18. Ibid.
19. Ibid.
20. Ibid., 32.

family. Initially her family "didn't really understand."[21] Her mother and grandmother traveled from Nashville to New York City to stage an intervention, prepared to redeem Dee from some unknown trauma.[22] They left New York upset and dismayed. Her mother felt she had failed to raise Dee properly, and Dee felt guilty for the pain her mother felt. For the subsequent two years, her family sent Rees cards and Bible verses until she insisted they stop. Eventually her family expressed their continued love for Rees even though they didn't understand her. Nevertheless, having Dee in their lives was ultimately more important to them than converting her from gay to straight. Rees stated, "I realized just as I had my own process, I think parents have their own process too. And it's about meeting them where they are and allowing them to have their time."[23]

Contrary to Alike in *Pariah*, Rees and her family chose love and togetherness over estrangement. Alike, played by Adepero Oduye, her overbearing religious mother, played by Kim Wayans, and her philandering father, played by Charles Parnell, reach a point of conflict and confrontation that results in the bright and artistic Alike leaving her New York City home for a high school on the West Coast where she would focus on writing poetry. One of the final scenes captures Alike reading her poem "I Am Not Broken, I Am Free" to her high school teacher who encouraged Alike to develop her gift of writing. Dee Rees embeds her original poem in the movie to give Alike a voice by which to embrace her identity as a black female lesbian. The last four lines of the poem are:

> Breaking is freeing
> Broken is freedom
> I am not broken
> I'm free.[24]

These lines, and the twenty that precede them, define freedom for Dee Rees. Using images that suggest struggle and pain

21. Ibid.
22. Ibid.
23. Ibid., 33.
24. Rees, *I Am Not Broken, I am Free—Pariah*, lines 21–24.

results in a new way of being in the world, Rees writes about the generative aspects of heartbreak. Light both breaks in and light breaks out from a broken Alike. From the painful breaking she is opened to light that enters in and she generates light that she releases. Light is love that shines in on her and radiates out from her. Her spirit, no longer trapped within her, ironically takes liberating flight because she is broken open. Being broken open is not brokenness or a fragmenting of the spirit, but a freeing of the spirit to be whole. Hope is symbolized as sunrise, new light, and possibilities, which are all phrases in the poem. These symbols of hope foreshadow flourishing for Alike who will live an authentic life. She will also shine a light of love and hope on all those she encounters. What about Alike's ability to shine love and hope on her family?

Prior to leaving New York City there is a scene in which Alike visits her mother at work to say goodbye. She finds her mother on break reading her Bible. Alike, with tears in her eyes, tells her mother that she loves her, only to watch her mother close her Bible, get up, and walk away from Alike without saying a word. This scene suggests the predominance of homophobia in the black church in contrast to love and forgiveness embodied in a black female lesbian teenager. Rees draws moviegoers' attention to the brokenness of the homophobic church that refuses to practice key Christian principles of unconditional love and acceptance and grace-filled forgiveness. While *Pariah* does not explicitly include scenes set in a church, there are explicit and implicit references to the church throughout the movie. When Alike's mother disapproves of her friendship with butch-looking girls, her mother encourages her to befriend Bina, a girl from church, played by Aasha Davis. While walking home from church Bina and Alike are introduced to each other by their mothers. The girls' relationship grows and Alike's mom is pleased they are spending lots of time together. However, Bina comes on to Alike as a same-gender-loving person. Alike loses her virginity with Bina during a sleepover together. The next morning Alike is devastated when Bina names what for her is the casual and noncommittal nature of their sexual encounter as well as their relationship. A subsequent scene between Bina and a teenage boy coming on to her in her bedroom suggests she too is in the natural phase of discovering her sexual identity as lesbian, straight, or bisexual. Interpretations of the tacit presence of the church suggest the denial of the presence of LGBT people in the church and Rees's indictment of hypocrisy within the Christian church. Although rendered invisible, LGBT people are present in the church. Also, many practices in congregations demonize LGBT people while exploiting their talents in the context of worship. Rees suggests the Christian church is indistinguishable from societal homophobia when its very nature and mission demands a clear distinction from culture.

Dee Rees subsequently reflected on her experience with black churches in her interview with *The Crisis* magazine. While she notes that black churches are not monolithic in their position on openly gay members, she acknowledges there are some churches who accept lesbian, gay, bisexual, and transgendered (LGBT) people and some that don't. Her own church experience has been of both. She was once a member of a church that appeared to accept LGBT people until "the pastor announced a program in which there would be testimonials from people who have been 'cured' of being gay."[25] She explained how hurtful it was to sit in the congregation hearing and seeing the horrible event, especially since she thought she had found a church community that had accepted her.[26] Rees "leaned on her spirituality to get her through the tough times with her family as she came to terms with her identity."[27] It is safe to conclude that her spirituality also sustained her even as she longed for a congregation that would accept her unconditionally. Her thoughts on spirituality reveal her personal freedom to live a seamless life as a sexual and spiritual person. She said:

> I realized that my spirituality and my sexuality aren't mutually exclusive. Some people assume because you're gay you must not be Christian. I'm like no. I'm Christian

25. Joiner, "Visible Lives," 34.

26. Ibid.

27. Ibid.

and I'm a lesbian. Once I was firm in the truth that God
loves me and God was with me, it didn't matter necessar-
ily what the church said.[28]

Her powerful words are prophetic. She proclaims God's presence and unconditional love for her regardless of the church and
its position on lesbian black women. She goes on to charge the
church with a more appropriate calling when she says, "At its best
I think the church should create a safe and loving space for all
people. It should be inclusive . . . and not separate people from
God. It should unite them with God."[29]

Dee Rees practices freedom through her beliefs about the
church and how God desires churches to act toward LGBT people.
Her reflections above are indicative of her self-awareness and her
relationship with God and others. She also exudes a sense of self
that defies the caustic homophobic environments found in some
congregations.

Rees is among like-minded screenwriters, directors, and
producers who are gay artists and are "using their talents to dispel myths and provide insights into the Black gay experience."[30]
Her insights on the Christian church mentioned above coupled
with her skillful critique of the church woven throughout *Pariah*
is consistent with an understanding of freedom sufficient for the
individual and the community.

Freedom as Emancipatory Hope

Freedom is a way of being in the world, a practice of moving toward what one hopes for, both materially and spiritually. It is body
and mind focused on things imagined. Freedom is striving for the
ultimate spiritual self and the community to thrive as liberated in
a way that defies spiritual, physical, and psychological weaken-
ing of the mind and body. Freedom as emancipatory hope means

28. Ibid.
29. Ibid.
30. Ibid., 30.

flourishing, particularly for the black/white mixed-race lesbian in whose body race, gender, and sexual orientation intersect.

There are two notions of freedom as emancipatory hope that should be considered by African-descended women and communities. The first is freedom that brings a liberating hope and that depends on a clear identity. Just as Michele Aboro is clear about who she is and how to maintain her authenticity, so too must African-descended women be clear and authentic about their identity. An authentic identity keeps one moored to one's core values, beliefs, and practices. It also sustains a person during stressful and stormy times in life. A key to thriving amid tumultuous environments of sexism, racism, and heteronormativity is an authentic identity.

Like the individual African-descended woman, institutions, such as congregations/churches, should also be anchored in an authentic identity. The benefits of doing so are similar to those experienced by individuals who practice an authentic identity and include consistent evidence of core values and beliefs reflected in ministries. Obviously individual members with authentic identities shape such congregations. The Rev. James Forbes was senior pastor at Riverside Church in New York City when the congregation unapologetically declared its unconditional acceptance of LGBT people.[31] This public confession of the congregation's practices signaled not only to the city of New York but to people around the globe that their identity was focused on social justice. Visitors to New York City find their way to Riverside because its authentic identity is solidified in the practice of receiving all people who enter its walls and standing with all people for their liberty and justice.

Second, freedom as emancipatory hope results in the thriving of African-descended women and their communities when they have agency. Freedom for personal agency is generally understood. More specifically, freedom leads to flourishing—where marginalized black women and girls have agency to develop resources for economic, political, and social stability and are enabled

---

31. Mosbacher and Reid, *All God's Children.*

"to participate on a par with nonpoor peers."[32] Keri Day offers deep insights on agency for poor black women that empowers them to thrive when they have equitable access to resources:[33] affordable housing, healthcare, and jobs. These resources offer a living wage and opportunities for professional development. The Poor People's Campaign (PPC), led by the black church, is her model. She argues "that black churches can resurrect and redeem the PPC movement by promoting the image of *prosperity as the interplay between individual fulfillment and communal thriving*."[34] She goes on to say: "Individual fulfillment and communal well-being are thus inextricably related."[35] African-descended women and their communities thrive when avenues to resources are open and their ability to solve problems and create marketable products is honored.

There are a few congregations that provide ministries that attend to the flourishing of such African-descended women and communities. Day mentions City of Refuge in San Francisco where the Rev. Bishop Yvette Flunder is the senior pastor. This congregation provides social justice missions that address structural issues of poverty while also providing an environment for same-gender–loving persons to flourish in a congregation that nurtures their spirituality "by promoting a more loving, compassionate theology."[36] The Riverside Church, mentioned above, now led by senior minister Rev. Amy K. Butler, is another example of a congregation whose social justice missions address systemic injustices that oppress and marginalize people because of their race/ethnicity, gender, sexual orientation, and nationality. Also among this group of congregations is St. John's "Downtown" United Methodist Church in Houston, Texas, where Revs. Juanita and Rudy Rasmus are the pastors. The congregation's social justice missions not only address systems of oppression but also empower leadership in the congregation and city of Houston from among those who have

32. Day, *Unfinished Business*, 5.
33. Ibid., 123.
34. Ibid., 122.
35. Ibid.
36. Ibid., 122–23.

been homeless and rendered invisible because they are lesbian or gay. Their motto "We Love You and There is Nothing You Can Do About It" is embodied in every worship service where hugs and handshakes supersede name and status and every ministry seeks to promote personal and communal flourishing.

While there are other notions of freedom as emancipatory hope for African-descended women and their communities in addition to an authentic identity and agency, this chapter showed two concrete ways of thinking about freedom as discussed above. Freedom is so inextricably related to a liberating hope that it is difficult to argue the concept apart from hope. Nevertheless, the intent was to focus on freedom as revealed in the lives of black/ white mixed-race and African American lesbians that gives new ideas about the priceless gift of freedom that only God, through the power of the Holy Spirit, can provide.

The next chapter explores this relationship between emancipatory hope and the Holy Spirit in a purportedly post-racial society. It considers the work of the Holy Spirit from lessons learned from the lives of black/white mixed-race young women about forgiveness, femaleship, fortitude, and freedom discussed in chapters 1–4.

5

Emancipatory Hope
and the Holy Spirit

HOW CAN AFRICAN-DESCENDED WOMEN, particularly black/white mixed-race young women, hope in an allegedly but not actually post-racial society? In this chapter I suggest that the kind of hope that can truly liberate us from the interlocking and pervasive oppressions of racism, classism, sexism, and heterosexism comes through a process of forgiveness, fellowship/femaleship, fortitude, and freedom and that for Christian women it is the empowerment of the Holy Spirit that makes it possible for us to hope for such liberation.

We despair because of being marginalized for our race, ethnicity, economic status, sexual orientation, and/or other causes of injustice. Those who marginalize us are the economically, politically, and socially powerful men and women. Emancipatory hope imagines and expects the dismantling of systems of domination that include racism, sexism, classism, and heterosexism. Thanks to emancipatory hope, we grab hold of God's vision of personal and communal transformation from systemic causes of despair and can become agents rather than victims of our futures. Such hope comes from the Holy Spirit, the advocate and comforter, the one who will be with us always, to the end of time.

This chapter explores how the Holy Spirit is at work in the world today bringing about emancipatory hope in a purportedly post-racial era—a sociohistorical period that supposedly ignores race and racial identity in pursuit of a colorblind society.[1] The Holy Spirit empowers the people of God to usher in emancipatory hope and hope for a different future. The Holy Spirit empowers us to be co-partners with God in this, a society in which post-racial ideals are incompatible with contemporary racial practices. Race does matter in economic, social, and political negotiations in North American society. The United States is far from being a post-racial country when scores of black children are killed annually at the hands of racist citizens and law officers and political candidates send implicit messages about the racial/ethnic groups they will marginalize when they are in power. To be clear, the first seventeen years of the twenty-first century in the United States are not indicative of a color-blind climate despite all the noise and hype about it being a post-racial period. This has to change. We have to change it, together.

Just as change finds strength in numbers, so in this chapter I enlist another scholar to think with me about a post-racial society and the Holy Spirit. My conversation with Dr. Karen Baker-Fletcher, womanist systematic theologian and author of *Dancing with God: The Trinity from a Womanist Perspective,* is woven throughout this chapter. I asked her about a post-racial United States and the experiences of black/white mixed-race young women. She responded first by referring to a poem she had written.

> KBF: This is from *Sisters of Dust, Sisters of Spirit.* It's called, "The Pomegranate." I started the poem when I was in college and I didn't complete it until somewhere between 1995 and 1998. In the 1990s there was a book published entitled *The Color of Water.* Its influence ended up in the poem as well, [but] that book was not available when I was a college student in the late 1970s when I started writing the poem.

Some mothers say God is the color of water, true

1. Wise, *Colorblind*, 24.

Others the color of air, true

Some mothers say God is the color of fire, true

Others the color of earth, true

>One may split a pomegranate open for a daughter seeking what is true, what makes us human

What makes "God," God to admire its beauty inside out?

Its jewels bled and the seeds flew

>The daughter cried and the mother rocked, whispering, "Skins are meant to be kept on, housing the beauty that keeps them rosy, breathing the secret that makes them glow that warms our hearts, delights us holy

'Let God be God' said the mother, wiping the daughter's tears:

'The color of coffee beans, your sister

The color of wet sand, your brother

The color of blanched almonds, your mother

The color of Georgia clay, your father

Glory, the color of God

Glory, the secret within.'

Now, I don't think we're living in a post-racial world. Human beings have a very hard time thinking of difference positively, whether it's different colors or different hair textures or different facial features or even heights and weights and all of those things. The Holy Spirit, *pneuma*, is from a word that means "breath" or "wind," and who has seen the wind? And so this poem is about God but for me it also applies to the Holy Spirit . . . it's the color of glory—of every imaginable color and unimaginable color. Colors we have never even seen are the color of God, the color of the Holy Spirit. And God embraces it all, though we don't as human beings. And biracial young adults have a hard time because the black race, as Alice Walker says in her definition of womanist, is like a flower garden with every color in it . . . and among biracial children we find every color. They may be the color of their black parent, they may be the color of their white or Hispanic parent. They may be a color in the range between the two. They may be the color of their black parent's grandmother . . . and they are a part of that flower garden [that Alice Walker wrote about in *Inheriting our Mother's Garden*]. So the Holy Spirit may be the color of glory, but we humans come in many, many colors and we still don't treat each other well.

. . . [R]ace is a complex issue. I don't know if that means [that people] living in a post-racial society . . . ignore the beauty of all of our colors as human beings, it does not mean a color-blind society—that's the opposite of dismantling systems of oppression. It is embracing all of our colors as beautiful, it is embracing our humanity, . . . the humanity that is in our eyes that glows through the skin, that secret within [that] I talk about in the poem "The Pomegranate," you know, the skin is meant to be kept on, it's not to be ignored. It's not something to be ashamed of. It's not something to be frustrated about. It's something to be loved and embraced, and when we love and embrace one another in all of our colors and shapes and sizes and features and hair textures, that's my emancipatory hope—that we do that! And that's the hope I believe the Holy Spirit is calling us into. A [world in which] the biracial child won't have to be ashamed of being black and white—because they're both good! And they're both beautiful and they're both loveable and they're both loved by God. God has created us just as we are in these bodies, in these skins . . . with our hair textures . . . . Emancipatory hope is just seeing that realized, and sometimes we see it realized in moments in society and in church. I think we have a ways to go though.

Baker-Fletcher's reflections on a society that is not yet postracial sets the tone for discourse on the Holy Spirit. While the Holy Spirit is the color of glory metaphorically, in contrast, as Baker-Fletcher reminds us, black/white mixed-race young women have many physical colors ranging from black or dark brown to white. And they live in a society where the hue of your skin can have life-or-death consequences. Skin color matters in a racist society. Dark skin tones surface hatred for black people as well as pose a threat to and elicit fear from those who harbor stereotypes and prejudices against dark-skinned people. Even within the African American community, internalized racism results in color biases whereby some people value lighter skin tones more than darker ones.[2]

While black/white mixed-race young women are the colors of a garden, the Holy Spirit, who breathes on the garden is the color of glory. Who is the Holy Spirit? And how does the Holy Spirit empower an emancipatory hope in a racist society? We turn to the Bible for help with this.

When his ascension was imminent, Jesus spoke to his disciples about the kingdom of God and admonished them to stay in Jerusalem until the Holy Spirit came upon them as promised by the Father (Acts 1:1–5). He contrasted the baptism by water that John did with the upcoming baptism with the Holy Spirit (verse 5). His disciples were concerned about the restoration of the kingdom to Israel. They obviously still did not understand his teaching about the reign of God nor did they realize the extraordinary experience that was forthcoming. Reiterating the coming of the Holy Spirit, Jesus replies to their concern in Acts 1:7–8.

> It is not for you to know the times or periods that the Father has set by his own authority. But you will receive power when the Holy Spirit has come upon you; and you will be my witnesses in Jerusalem, in all Judea and Samaria, and to the ends of the earth.

He redirects their attention away from their anxieties to the power that they will receive from the Holy Spirit who will be with them after his ascension, as God promised earlier. The disciples will be invincible in revealing and spreading the ethos of Jesus to all the world.

The Holy Spirit is the third person of the Godhead, the Trinity or Triune God. God is Spirit dynamically related to the three agents in the Godhead.[3] God the Father/Mother or Parent, and God the Logos/Word/Son incarnate in Jesus the Christ or the anointed one, are the other two agents in the Trinity.[4] They are one

2. Parker, *Trouble Don't Last Always*, 74–75.

3. Baker-Fletcher, *Dancing with God*, 54–55.

4. Ibid., 57–61.

in substance, according to Western Christian thought and belief.[5] The Holy Spirit participates in the life of God the Father and Son, "a life of mutual relationship grounded in the understanding of God as relational community,"[6] as Karen Baker-Fletcher argues.

In the Gospel of John, we find passages that identify the Holy Spirit as the Advocate (John 14:15b, 22a, 15:26a, and 16:7) who will be with the disciples. Some Bible translations call the Spirit the Comforter instead. In addition to Advocate, the Amplified Bible (AMP) uses the noun Helper and parenthetically includes other synonyms of Comforter, like Intercessor-Counselor, Strengthener, and Standby.[7] All these indicate how the Holy Spirit works in the lives of followers of Christ. John 14:18 states: "I will not leave you orphaned, I am coming to you." Jesus signals his presence with his beloved disciples as being the Spirit. Rudolf Bultmann argues that, "Since the gift of the Spirit was brought about by the salvation-occurrence accomplished in Christ, the Spirit can be regarded as God's and also as Christ's gift, hence one may also speak of the 'Spirit of Christ' or 'of the Lord.'"[8]

The power of the Holy Spirit begins with the indwelling presence of the Spirit. Where does the Spirit of Christ dwell? The Holy Spirit dwells within our bodies and simultaneously in the world fighting the spiritual forces of evil on our behalf. First Corinthians 3:16 states:

> Do you not know that you are God's temple and that God's Spirit dwells in you? If anyone destroys God's temple, God will destroy that person. For God's temple is holy, and you are that temple.

Paul admonishes disciples of Jesus Christ like us on ways to care for the Holy Spirit that dwells within us. Galatians 5:16 cautions us about the difference between what our flesh desires

---

5. Ibid., 55.

6. Ibid., 57.

7. Amplified Bible (AMP), https://www.biblegateway.com/passage/?search=John+14%3A26&version=AMP.

8. Bultmann, *Theology of the New Testament*, 153.

and what the Spirit of God desires that dwells within us. "The fruit of the Spirit is love, joy, peace, patience, kindness, generosity, faithfulness, gentleness and self-control." These practices are not easy. Paul himself, the letter writer to the Corinthian and Galatian churches, admits the difficulty of allowing the Spirit of God that dwells within us to take control over our little spirit. To be clear, the Spirit of God dwells in our bodies as well as the institutional body, the church. Although sometimes our individual bodies as well as the institutional body of Christ grieve the Holy Spirit with actions contradictory to the desires of God. We who have taken on Jesus Christ as our savior struggle daily with our desires of the flesh that wage war against the Spirit that dwells within us. Addictions that overcome the indwelling Spirit in favor of the human spirit lead to destruction. Deceitfulness, unfaithfulness, and plotting the demise of a person or group are all desires of the little spirit or our flesh. Our individual struggle each day is to allow the indwelling Holy Spirit to overcome our fleshly desires.

The Spirit of God dwells in our bodies and our bodies make up the institutional body, the church. The institutional body of Christ grieves the Holy Spirit with actions contradictory to the desires of God. Sometimes our collective desires of the flesh cause havoc in our communities of faith, the church, suppressing and oppressing and grieving the Spirit of God that dwells in the church. When churches fail to stand up and speak truth to political powers, the little spirit is in control and not the Holy Spirit. When churches fail to be prophetic as well as pious, then the Holy Spirit is being suppressed. Dr. King wrote that, "As the chief moral guardian of the community, the church must implore men/women to be good and well-intentioned and must extol the virtues of kindheartedness and conscientiousness."[9] The church should never tire of reminding men/women/boys/girls that they have a moral responsibility to be intelligent in the face of ignorant people who legislate ignorant policies. When the Holy Spirit is suppressed and oppressed in the church, the church loses its distinctive and prophetic voice. The

9. King, *Strength to Love*, 9.

church has no power if the church does not yield to the indwelling Holy Spirit.

The Spirit of God, in unity with God the Parent and God the Son, "empowers and encourages the dance . . . of life."[10] This desire of the Spirit harmonizes with God's promises of abundant life for all who believe and trust that God has not forgotten them even as they suffer. "The distinctive action of the Holy Spirit is to comfort or console, to heal, encourage, and empower,"[11] states Baker-Fletcher. In addition to Acts 1:8 quoted above, New Testament Scripture gives several references to the power of the Holy Spirit. Jesus was "filled with the power of the Spirit" (Luke 4:14a) as he returned to Galilee at the outset of his public ministry and read from Isaiah 61 in the synagogue of his hometown of Nazareth. The ability of the disciples to speak in other languages at Pentecost, Acts 2, was evidence of the power of the Holy Spirit that Jesus talked about in Acts 1:8. Paul prays for the church at Ephesus (Eph 3:16) that God "may grant that you may be strengthened in your inner being with power through his Spirit." In Paul's Letter to the Romans, he claims bragging rights to speak of his work with the Gentiles "by the power of the Spirit of God."[12] The Greek term "*pneuma* is the miraculous divine power that stands in absolute contrast to all that is human."[13] The Spirit manifests in inexplicable ways in the life of a Christian disciple that seem far beyond the capabilities and powers of a human being.[14] The Spirit of God gave power to the disciples to do miraculous things and will give power to Christians to act in contemporary society as if our hopes for ending racism will be realized in our lifetime. A key point here is that the Holy Spirit gives power to the people of God to bring hope into the lives of those who are oppressed.

Dr. Baker-Fletcher describes how the Holy Spirit acts as an empowering member of the Godhead in the world today. She

---

10. Baker-Fletcher, *Dancing with God*, 56.

11. Ibid.

12. Rom 15:19.

13. Baker-Fletcher, *Dancing with God*, 153.

14. Ibid.

places Mary the mother of Jesus at the center of her discussion as she talks about the Holy Spirit.

> KBF: In *Dancing with God* I have a section called the Holy Spirit and Mary the woman-bearer of God and I include the work of Diana Hayes who is a womanist Catholic theologian who has spent more time on Mary than most Protestant womanists. It's hard for me to think about the Holy Spirit without thinking of Mary the mother of God, Mary the one who bears Christ, who carries and births Christ into the world. Mary as a single mother was inspired to do so by the power of the Holy Spirit because the Spirit of God was upon her. It is the Spirit of God that was in her who conceived the child Jesus, the Son of God. Protestants have given little attention to Mary as *theotokos* or mother of God. Yet, the question about Mary's relationship to Christ was very important for the early church writers. Diana Hayes writes that Mary is, "too often seen as a docile, submissive woman," but that "Black Catholic womanists, instead, see a young woman sure of her God and her role in God's salvific plan." Hayes identifies Mary, mother of Jesus, as "a young, unwed pregnant woman [who] proclaims her allegiance with God and with her brothers and sisters with whom she lived, as a Jew under Roman oppression." She is not a symbol of passivity but a "courageous and outrageous authority" who gives "a prophetic 'yes' to God standing alone, yet empowered." And to me that is a womanist description of the power of the Holy Spirit inspiring and moving an unwed mother, and it is the Holy Spirit who makes this child that Mary conceives and that she courageously and audaciously bears and prophetically speaks about, the Son of God. However it happened, whatever happened, it is the Holy Spirit that makes it possible. And . . . I connect Mary's inspiration in the Holy Spirit with that of the baby who was born to Mamie Till-Mobley. That baby was Emmett Till. [Many years later] like Mary, she has to see her son, his mutilated beaten-drowned-swollen-bloated body barely recognizable except to her, because she was his mother. . . . And she is in despair and she is ready to take her own life and the phone rings and because of

that simple phone ring her thoughts of suicide are interrupted. And it comes to her after she has answered that phone and puts the phone down, she feels the Holy Spirit in her heart speaking to her, saying, "Just as my son Jesus was persecuted, crucified, wrongfully killed, and his life has meaning for the world, so the life of your son Emmett Till, will have meaning for the world." And she was in the Church of God in Christ, COGIC, a Pentecostal church, and so this woman knows the Holy Spirit. And so she listens to the Holy Spirit. And she became a very important leader in the very early years of the civil rights movement.

Baker-Fletcher describes the empowering work of the Holy Spirit in the pregnancy and birth of Jesus Christ to a poor unwed mother named Mary. She refers to Mamie Till-Mobley, the mother of Emmet Till, whom she compares to Mary. The Holy Spirit gave Mamie Till-Mobley power to reveal her son's lynched and desecrated body to the world as an act of justice for him and for all persons and their families who had experienced deadly hate crimes. The Holy Spirit gives power to work for justice in unimaginable ways and through the least expected people. Such courage is an essential gift that comes through the power of the Spirit of God.

> EP: So, in light of this human problem of not treating each other well, even though God has created a diverse population of people, that include black/white mix-raced young people—and I'm speaking specifically of girls—how do you see God acting to bring about hope for these young persons? And as you talk about that, give me your idea of what hope means and then I will follow up with my ideas about hope.

> KBF: I was very moved by a Perkins [School of Theology] chapel service we had in the fall [2014] and one of the student leaders was Lael Melville. And during that service she talked about micro-aggressions, and there was a diversity of students who held up posters, signs, with some of the things that people say that are micro-aggressions around issues of race and color and other

identity issues. But I was particularly interested by those around color. And I was moved by a woman who rose and spoke and held up a sign that said, "What are you?" That's a micro-aggression that biracial young girls experience . . . that they receive . . . "What are you?" And if they look white and identify as black they are criticized for that, which is another micro-aggression. . . . If . . . they're brown skinned or dark brown or blue-black and they don't identify as black, they say "I'm an American," or "I'm biracial," or "I'm like Tiger Woods," and I think he said he was Cablanasian, and then we have Raven Symone who has another way of describing herself but I can't remember how to say all of that. And then they're criticized on Facebook; you see people posting articles about what biracial or even African American young women of the younger generation have said about their identity, and some of the comments are very cruel. I'm not saying whether or *how* biracial young women should identify themselves, I'm just noticing the pain of criticism they received for whatever choice they make . . . .

But where I saw the hope was in that chapel service when the micro-aggressions were named and I think we need more opportunities for naming in community worship, in our churches, more opportunities like that.

EP: I have written that hope that is emancipatory is the expectation that oppression and hegemonic forces will be dismantled—

KBF: Yes!

EP: And that God, and we in partnership with God, are responsible for dismantling those types of systems of oppression. So emancipatory hope is the expectation that God, and we in partnership with God, will dismantle oppressive situations.

The Holy Spirit gives us power to be courageous as we work for justice in a racist, sexist, classist, and homophobic society.

While courage is not the only attribute that the Holy Spirit brings, it is essential for partnering with God to dismantle systemic oppression. When we are filled with the power of the Holy Spirit we receive other gifts from the indwelling Spirit of God such as those listed in Galatians 5:22–23. Courage, however, captures the persona of Jesus when he, though very human yet divine, confronted corrupt leaders and stood on behalf of marginalized people. Karen Baker-Fletcher responds with her perspective of courage that the Holy Spirit brings.

> KBF: I believe the Holy Spirit gives us the hope to speak our truth like Mamie Till-Mobley spoke her truth. She spoke her truth and she insisted that the world look at her son's face and body. It takes courage to do that. It takes courage to speak. It takes courage to name one's reality. Her movement from despair to hope came from the Holy Spirit. As a Church of God in Christ woman she knew where her hope came from. And [as it was for her, so for us] it's the Holy Spirit that gives us the courage to speak honestly about racism, sexism, heterosexism, colorism, and all of these issues. And so when we can't find strength in ourselves—[we take] a literal deep breath and listen to our own breath and pray for that breath of the Holy Spirit, then receive it, accept it, and just let in the Spirit, let the words of truth come forth, and the very breath of God that is in us, and we find that just by listening to our own breath and having a moment of silence [we can speak with courage.] We have to be patient sometimes with one another and have room for silence so we can breathe, so we can catch our literal breath, so that the breath of God can move our tongues to utter the truth that we need to utter without fear—and hope is the opposite of fear for me . . . and maybe that's why there's no fear in love—faith, hope, love (laughs), ya know? I wonder how those three work together in what we're talking about. I mean hope is a kind of faith. To me hope is a faith beyond faith because no matter what things look like it's a faith so strong you don't know where the courage is going to come from—it just comes. How do we teach that to young girls though?

EP: That would be the challenge. In my book I argue that emancipatory hope comes as a result of forgiveness, femaleship, fortitude, and freedom . . . so fortitude is really close to courage. Does courage presuppose something positive?

KBF: Very positive.

EP: So you're saying that you cannot have courage and do something negative . . . like use hate language or even abuse or exercise micro-aggression—that does not take courage—is that your point?

KBF: Yes, to me that's ignorance, cowardice, and when it's intentional, fear.

EP: So people respond out of fear not thinking through, but knowing what is life-giving, if you will, or what is right?

KBF: It takes courage, and courage is a kind of fortitude. And there's no courage without hope, ya know? So fortitude, courage, hope, they go together. [One must say] "on this ground I stand" or "we shall not be moved." It's taking a stand in the face of all odds, taking a stand for the good, taking a stand for what is just, taking a stand for what is righteous.

I think the body is very important [in this process of finding courage and hope]. I think that for young women, athletic sports, working out, dance, something like that, is very important for learning about courage and hope and fortitude . . . how we hold ourselves in a strong way. Learning through the body teaches the spirit just as much as learning through the [Holy] Spirit teaches the body. And all too often we separate the Spirit from the body, but I've noticed that for me I feel most spiritually strong when I have done a good workout. It changes my stance and the way I stand. It changes the stance of the young women that I see working out around me. I don't care if it's basketball or something else. It changes something on the inside. And so I think that hope and courage is about the body and how we see our bodies, not just in terms of the color of our bodies . . . but how we take care of our bodies because our bodies are the temple of the Holy Spirit. It takes confidence to get in there and play a basketball game, it takes courage, it takes hope. It's not just from the Bible that we learn about these things, it's not just in church. There are so many athletes who can tell the story of how being physically active gives them more confidence, courage, and hope, and to expect the best—the good—in life. And [we have] to share that with others and to motivate others—it's not just about sitting in a pew at church for me. That's never been good enough. And there's no way it's going to be good enough for young women.

While Baker-Fletcher believes that fortitude and courage are similar in meaning, her main point in this last segment is the importance of girls becoming physically fit and having a healthier body image and self-image in order to nurture their courage and hope. Nevertheless, she clearly associates courage with the Holy Spirit that dwells within our bodies.

Dr. Martin Luther King Jr. said that courage is one of the supreme virtues known to humankind.[15] He goes on to lift up philosophers that included Thomas Aquinas who said that courage is the strength of mind capable of conquering whatever threatens the attainment of the highest good. Dr. King contrasted courage and cowardice when he wrote:

> Courage is an inner resolution to go forward in spite of the obstacles and frightening situations; cowardice is a submissive surrender to circumstance. Courage breeds creative self-affirmation; cowardice produces destructive self-abnegation. Courage faces fear and thereby masters it; cowardice represses fear and is thereby mastered by it. Courageous men/women never lose the zest for living even though their life situation is zestless. Cowardly

15. King, *Strength to Love*, 122.

men/women, overwhelmed by the uncertainties of life, lose the will to live.[16]

Although Dr. King does not mention the presence of the Holy Spirit with respect to the gift of courage, as a civil rights advocate he faced many deadly situations that only the Holy Spirit could have given him the courage to withstand. As stated above, the Holy Spirit gives power to the people of God to bring hope into the lives of those who are oppressed, themselves included. Dr. King was an exemplar of that hope. As it did for him, so too for us the Holy Spirit gives power to hope for liberation from interlocking oppressions of racism, classism, sexism, and heterosexism through a process of forgiveness, fellowship/femaleship, fortitude, and freedom.

The Spirit Gives Power to Forgive

Jesus, who received the Holy Spirit in bodily form like a dove at his baptism, carried out his ministry in the power of the Holy Spirit. "Jesus, full of the Holy Spirit, returned from the Jordan and was led by the Spirit in the wilderness, where for forty days he was tempted by the devil" (Luke 4:1–2a). This Scripture is one among many that is evidence of the Spirit indwelling and leading Jesus. The Spirit gave Jesus power to heal the sick and to raise Lazarus from the dead. Ultimately, it was the Spirit that gave Jesus power to forgive those who crucified him. "When they came to the place that is called the Skull, they crucified Jesus there with the criminals, one on his right and one on his left. Then Jesus said, "Father, forgive them; for they do not know what they are doing" (Luke 23:33–34a). As we saw in chapter 1, forgiveness is the intentional effort to restore broken relationships. The forgiveness that Jesus practiced was essential to restoring his fractured relationships. After Jesus was united with Peter who had denied him on three different occasions. His reception of and interaction with Peter demonstrated that he had forgiven Peter. Jesus modeled what he had taught Peter during their ministry together when he asked

16. Ibid., 124.

Jesus how often he should forgive a member of the church who sins against him. Jesus admonished Peter and us to forgive seventy times seven (Matt 18:21–22).

Dr. King coupled forgiveness with love when he wrote: "He who is devoid of the power to forgive is devoid of the power to love."[17] King makes the case that the act of forgiving must be initiated by the one who has been injured by some great wrong or tortuous injustice. Such a mandate for human victims can only be powered by the Holy Spirit.

Black/white mixed-race young women who have experienced harm or injury by other women need the power of the Holy Spirit in order to be able to forgive. Indeed, all of us whose relationships have been shattered need the power of the Holy Spirit to glue our relationships back together through forgiveness. The Spirit gives us the gift of relationality that must be maintained by forgiving our debtors just as the Spirit forgives us our debts (Matt 6:12). The process of forgiving begins with praying as Jesus taught us in word and disposition. Prayer coupled with consistent efforts to restore a relationship leads to forgiveness. Within the process of forgiveness, women, particularly black/white mixed-race young women, can form healthy relationships with other young women that will evolve into femaleship. The Spirit gives power for women to exercise femaleship just as Jesus exercised fellowship. Femaleship is deep connection among women synonymous with communion with God, self, and others.

Jesus shared meals and conversation with a number of different people who were different from him. Jesus fellowshipped with his friends, the disciples as well as with women, tax collectors, lepers, and religious leaders. His fellowship with the disciples during meals was institutionalized into the Eucharist for all disciples of Jesus Christ to celebrate in memory of his life, death, and resurrection. It was during the last supper, a significant event of fellowship with the disciples, that Jesus foreshadowed his betrayal by one of his disciples. It was also during the event of eating a meal together with his disciples after his resurrection that Jesus fellowshipped

17. King, *Strength to Love*, 44.

with his disciples. The risen Lord broke bread and drank from the cup with Peter who had denied him three times. Surely through this act of fellowship Jesus was acknowledging his forgiveness of Peter.

Black/white mixed-race young women who are Christians engage in the practice of femaleship when they, like Jesus, share a meal as an act of forgiveness. Indeed it is difficult, if not impossible, to share a meal with someone who has brought you harm. Moving beyond the hurt from a fractured relationship to acknowledge that forgiveness through a common meal and conversation is femaleship. The Holy Spirit gives women power to mend or reconnect a broken relationship through the sharing of a meal. While the sharing over a brunch, lunch, or dinner maybe strained after the injured woman has forgiven the woman who injured her, it is the first step toward femaleship.

The Holy Spirit empowers femaleship—communion with God, self, and others—not only through the sharing of a common meal but also through playing together. Spa dates and girlfriend cruises are examples of playing together evidenced in joyous laughter. Likewise, women who pray together commune with each other and the Holy Spirit in a manner that surpasses human understanding. The "Spirit helps us in our weakness, for we do not know how to pray as we ought, but that very Spirit intercedes with sighs too deep for words" (Rom 8:26). The prayers of women are strengthened by critical Bible study. The Holy Spirit teaches us (John 14:26b) how to live in communion with other women as we study Scripture. The combination of play, prayer, and Bible study shape healthy and deep connections among women that leads to femaleship. Communion among women is fertile soil for shaping women of fortitude—the unfaltering resolve and strength of mind to stay the course for justice and righteousness no matter the challenge.

The Spirit Gives Power for Women to Show Fortitude

The best example of fortitude was modeled by Jesus when he was tempted by the devil. The account of the temptations of Jesus are bracketed with declarations of the Holy Spirit (Luke 4:1 and 14) indwelling and empowering him. The devil tempted him for forty days as he resolved to eat nothing. Attacking Jesus where he was most vulnerable, the devil taunted him, daring that he would use his power for human gratification. When Jesus responded by quoting Scripture, the devil rebutted also using Scripture. Yet Jesus never yielded to his human needs and desires, but persevered in the power of the Holy Spirit to resist the temptations of the devil. Jesus shows us that fortitude generated by the Holy Spirit prepares us spiritually to overcome any personal human challenges.

Women who exercise the resolve to press forward for the cause of a just society for all women and girls show fortitude. Key to the practice of fortitude is divine will that is more powerful than personal human will. By divine will I mean a spirituality like that of Jesus Christ. Central to his ability to overcome the temptations of his human will was his yielding to the power of the indwelling Spirit. The Spirit gave Jesus the capacity to practice spiritual disciplines of fasting and recitation of Scripture. These resulted in a spirituality that propelled his fortitude in just ministry for the marginalized and disenfranchised. Thus, the practice of spiritual disciplines of fasting, meditation/silence, the study of Scripture, prayer, speaking the truth, and other spiritual disciplines prepares us to show fortitude when we are faced with personal challenges as well as challenges in our work for justice. Fortitude is evidenced in freedom—the ontological ideal, a way of being in the world that defies the hard spiritual, physical, and psychological realities that so commonly enervate the minds and bodies of women.

The Spirit Gives Power for Women to be Free.

Freedom is the mental capacity to do good justice work with integrity while faced with daunting challenges.

Jesus carried out his entire ministry with a free mind-set. He never allowed religious and governmental authorities to dissuade him from living out his beliefs in unconditional love and a preference for the poor. Being fully human and divine, Jesus, the incarnate one of the Triune God, modeled a multitude of ways to live and work in freedom. He spoke truth to religious leaders who eventually plotted his murder and death because he challenged their traditions. He valued the flourishing of human beings when he healed the sick and fed the hungry as well as cared for the grieving. He used his powers to perform miracles indiscriminately for the poor as well as for the rich and powerful. He taught his followers how to do ministry in like manner. He was the essence of an excellent teacher, giving insight to problem-solving through the use of parables/case studies and modeling good leadership. He was a companion and an advocate for women from all backgrounds.

Women who live in freedom as they do the good work of justice must emulate Jesus Christ. The Holy Spirit gives women power to live in freedom to do the work of ministry. The capacity to have a free mind-set while doing ministries of advocacy for women and girls involves three components: First, women must rid themselves of internalized sexism. Women who despise other women because of the lack of critical self-reflection on detrimental beliefs about women and girls cannot be advocates for women and girls. Second, women must engage in lifelong learning about ways to advocate on behalf of women and girls. Critical reflection on changing laws and practices that impact the lives of women and girls is essential for advocacy work. Lastly, women must replenish their bodies and spirits periodically. Advocacy work in a female-demonizing culture requires ongoing self-care. These three ways that women can live in freedom are not an exhaustive list but are essential for women who advocate on behalf of other women and girls.

In this chapter I have argued that hope that truly liberates us from the interlocking and pervasive oppressions of racism, classism, sexism, and heterosexism comes through a process of forgiveness, femaleship, fortitude, and freedom and that for Christian women it is the empowerment of the indwelling presence of Holy Spirit that makes it possible for us to hope for such liberation. I have focused primarily on the experiences of African-descended women, specifically black/white mixed-raced young women. However, the pathway to a liberating hope, emancipatory hope, through forgiveness, femaleship, fortitude, and freedom is not exclusive to African-descended women. It is available to all women who desire to embody emancipatory hope.

Forgiveness, femaleship, fortitude, and freedom are not intended to be linear and lock-stepped. Women's relationships do not always begin with a need to forgive. A woman can enter into the process of realizing emancipatory hope that is relevant for her experiences whether the point of entry is the need to exercise fortitude or offer the gift of forgiveness to someone. And the process toward emancipatory is not exclusive to black/white mixed-race young women, but relevant for all women concerned about liberation from interlocking oppressions.

How can African-descended women, particularly black/white mixed-race young women, hope in an allegedly but not actually post-racial society? They carry within their bodies a four-hundred-year history of racial struggle between black and white people in North American society. They may resist out of awareness of the pervasive nature of racial and gender inequity. The problem is compounded when black/white mixed-race young women are unaware that they are the targets of bigotry, discrimination, prejudice, and even hate. This history influences the quality of their relationships regardless of their awareness of racial and gender discrimination in explicit or implicit forms. Their relationships with other women in particular are uniquely impacted in ways that draw attention to the matter.

Black/white mixed-race young women who are Christian hope for a future emancipated of interlocking and pervasive oppressions of racism, classism, sexism, and heterosexism, through the indwelling power of the Holy Spirit. They and other Christian women are empowered to embody the process of forgiveness, femaleship, fortitude, and freedom through the power of the Spirit.

This process restores and nurtures wholesome relationships between black/white mixed-raced young women and other women who are white or who are racial minorities. The Holy Spirit empowers the process of forgiveness, femaleship, fortitude, and freedom that springs forth from an emancipatory hope as we anticipate a better world of justice, love and peace.

> [Such] hope does not disappoint us, because God's love
> has been poured into our hearts through the Holy Spirit
> that has been given to us. Romans 5:5b

Conclusion

Horizons of Hope for Mixed-Race
Young Women and Girls

The process of emancipatory hope that involves forgiveness, femaleship, fortitude, and freedom is applicable to all women and girls who seek to transform their tragic relationships with other women and girls into healthy life-giving relationships. In this book, the tragic relationships of black/white mixed-race girls found in memoirs, movies, novels, and documentaries have functioned as "case studies" for arguing the pathway to emancipatory hope. So, what is the significance of emancipatory hope for ministry in Christian congregations that have mixed-race young women and girls? What is the vision for ministry with mixed-race girls whose parents are African, Latin, Asian, or Native American and European descendants? How can a congregation bear witness to its identity as a church that acts with courage through the power of the Holy Spirit to usher in a post-racial society? How can Christian congregations attend to the process of forgiveness, fellowship/femaleship, fortitude, and freedom? Concluding remarks for *Between Sisters: Emancipatory Hope out of Tragic Relationships* challenge Christian congregations to be reflective about their practices and construct new forms of ministry that attend to offering hope to the community of faith. A fitting starting point to answer the above questions is clarification of the nature of the Christian church that embodies emancipatory hope.

The church was created to be a beacon of hope in a hopeless world for marginalized people. Created as a movement of Jesus Christ, the Christian church is charged to practice the hope that Jesus modeled in his ministry. He proclaimed his mission in Nazareth when he read from the prophet Isaiah, "The Spirit of the Lord is upon me, because he has anointed me to bring good news to the poor. He has sent me to proclaim release to the captives and recovery of sight to the blind, to let the oppressed go free, to proclaim the year of the Lord's favor" (Luke 4:18). His ministry focused on hope for the marginalized, regardless of their social, political, and economic status. The Gospels indicate that many who followed Jesus experienced marginalization because of their gender, health, economic status, and social status as outcasts. To those who followed him, Jesus brought hope of moving from the margins of society to a life of flourishing, abundant life (John 10:10b). In the aftermath of his crucifixion, resurrection, and ascension, his disciples fought back hopelessness as they anticipated the promise of the Advocate, the Holy Spirit (John 14:15–17). The creation of the church at Pentecost (Acts 2) showed evidence of the hope that the group of marginalized followers had as they became the first Christians who were now marginalized because of their belief in and loyalty to a political and religious criminal of the Roman Empire.

The Acts of the Apostles describes the growth of the early Jesus movement. His disciples, certain women, his mother and brothers, fearing the religious and political authorities, waited in Jerusalem in an upstairs room of a house constantly praying as they anticipated the promise of baptism with the Holy Spirit. The group of about 120 (Acts 1:15b) were the first of the "early Jesus movement in the ancient Mediterranean world."[1] The movement increased to more than 3,000 persons (Acts 2:41) following Peter's

---

1. Bae, "Being and Becoming Church: The Spirit-Filled Genesis," https://www.oikoumene.org/en/resources/documents/assembly/2013-busan/bible-studies/being-and-becoming-church-the-spirit-filled-genesis, 12.

powerful proclamation at Pentecost. The young church devoted itself to the apostles' teaching, fellowship, praying, and sharing all their material possessions among all the members of the church (Acts 2:42–47). The apostles continue Jesus' practices of healing those who were crippled, blind, or suffered from other marginalized conditions. The apostles and the first Christians practiced a liberating hope, following the example of Jesus Christ through the indwelling Holy Spirit, for all marginalized people. Luke, the writer of Acts, "presents the Holy Spirit as the vitalizing enabler for creative and courageous Christian witness . . . the first Christians who, empowered by the Holy Spirit, defied the gravity of geographical, cultural, political, and spiritual restrictions with astounding inner strength, both individual and communal, to become witnesses of Jesus Christ (Acts 1:8)."[2] The early church, "the first faith community of Jesus' disciples" was conceived "as a Spirit-filled prophetic community, practicing justice and love."[3] Thus, the Christian church at its inception was a community of faith devoted to practices that brought about hope for all who joined the Jesus movement. Likewise, the contemporary Christian community of faith was created to give emancipatory hope for marginalized people who struggled against systemic oppression.

The Christian community of faith as a Spirit-filled prophetic community must offer a liberating hope through its practices of justice for all including black/white mixed-raced young women. Indeed, "[j]ustice gives rise to hope."[4] It is justice that people seek when they struggle against interlocking oppressions of racism, classism, sexism and heterosexism. Such oppressions cause tensions within families and within the church. Hope must be existentially relevant for all members of a congregation and "motivated by justice."[5] Like the first church, contemporary churches must practice "mutual accountability and responsibility, and . . .

2. Ibid., 15–17.

3. Ibid.

4. Sims, Powe, and Hill, *Religio-Political Narratives in the United States*, 112.

5. Ibid.

courage to differ and to resist the existing oppressive and unjust norms and values of society."[6] Hope flows out of prophetic communities of faith that work for justice for all who are oppressed, both within and beyond the faith community, especially for black/white mixed-race, biracial, young women and girls. A pathway to emancipatory hope through acts of justice is the church, empowered by the Holy Spirit, which models the process of forgiveness, femaleship, fortitude, and freedom.

The Spirit Gives Power to the Church to Forgive

When a church practices forgiveness, it engages in the process of moving away from overwhelming hurt or pain while holding accountable the perpetrators of the injustice.[7] African American congregations whose churches have been burned to the ground by white supremacists, but nonetheless moved beyond the situation to rebuild their religious edifices, are empowered by the Spirit to forgive and move on to rebuild their churches. The congregation of Mother Emanuel AME Church in Charleston, South Carolina engaged in the process of forgiveness after the massacre of their pastor and eight members of the church by a white supremacist during Bible study on June 17, 2015. The congregation showed forgiveness to the lone white gunman amid their unspeakable grief and pain. Churches like Mother Emanuel model forgiveness like Jesus Christ and therefore usher in a liberating hope for the members of the congregation.

In like manner, churches must seek forgiveness of their sins from those they have hurt and become accountable for the injustice that they have caused. Congregations who demonize queer women and men out of homophobic beliefs and practices should seek forgiveness if they are sincere about an identity of being a Spirit-filled prophetic community. Such churches must model

---

6. Bae, "Being and Becoming Church," 81–83.

7. Marshall, "Communal Dimensions of Forgiveness," 53.

forgiveness as well as seek forgiveness as an act of justice toward emancipatory hope that is best exemplified by Jesus Christ.

Jesus, who received the Holy Spirit in bodily form like a dove at his baptism, carried out his ministry in the power of the Holy Spirit. "Jesus, full of the Holy Spirit, returned from the Jordan and was led by the Spirit in the wilderness, where for forty days he was tempted by the devil" (Luke 4:1-2a). This Scripture is one among many that is evidence of the Spirit indwelling and leading Jesus. The Spirit gave Jesus power to heal the sick and to raise Lazarus from the dead. It was also the Spirit that gave Jesus power to forgive those who crucified him. "When they came to the place that is called The Skull, they crucified Jesus there with the criminals, one on his right and one on his left. Then Jesus said, 'Father, forgive them; for they do not know what they are doing'" (Luke 23:33–34a). As noted above, Dr. King coupled forgiveness with love when he wrote: "He who is devoid of the power to forgive is devoid of the power to love."[8]

Black/white mixed-race young women who have experienced harm or injury from their mothers, sisters, brothers, fathers, or anyone need the power of the Holy Spirit to forgive and the example of their congregation to forgive or seek forgiveness. In order to set such an example, congregations must ask themselves:

How is forgiveness woven into all aspects of worship, including sermons, litanies, prayers, music, as well as daily practices of governance in the life of the congregation?

How do the church teach members talk about biblical and theological perspectives on forgiveness?

How is forgiveness intentionally modeled by pastors and judicatory leaders, families and individuals?

How does a congregation seek forgiveness of marginalized and oppressed people when the church has been silent as they were persecuted?

Why must the church ask forgiveness from black/white mixed-race young women? As the Spirit enables us to forgive, so too the Spirit gives power to the church for femaleship.

8. Marshall, "Communal Dimensions of Forgiveness," 44.

The Spirit Gives Power to the Church for Femaleship

The word *femaleship*, as indicated in chapter 2, is a term that captures relationships among women and the Triune God. Femaleship is the sacredness of relationships among women and girls that is like divine communion, guided by the Holy Spirit. When a church practices femaleship, the community of faith engages in divine communion among its members that honors the equality of women to men. Women are created in the *imago dei*, in the image of God, just as men are. Both women and men have the potential for goodness and righteousness in the likeness of God the Creator. Through femaleship the church affirms women as leaders in the congregation and makes room for ministries specific to the needs of women and girls, ministries that honor their divine communion, and promote healthy relationships among women.

Jesus is the best exemplar of divine communion with all people regardless of their social location. He shared meals and conversations with numerous people who were different from him (see page 111). His intimate relationships included women as well as the twelve disciples. There were women disciples in addition to the twelve that followed him and who had a close relationship with him. The Gospel of Luke records the women disciples and discusses three of them, Mary Magdalene, Joanna, and Susanna. They were three of several "female traveling evangelists who made up the band of female workers who surrendered and sacrificed everything to follow Jesus."[9] The women disciples taught and recruited new believers as well as cooked the food, mended clothes, and donated their money to the ministry of Jesus.[10]

Mary Magdalene was healed of her illness, imagined as demon-possession, during first-century Palestine. She proved herself a capable leader among the women, and was "articulate, loyal, and persuasive."[11] The Gospels of Luke and John record her following Jesus during his ministry as well as during his trial, crucifixion,

9. Weems, *Just A Sister Away*, 87.
10. Ibid., 87.
11. Ibid., 89.

and also during his resurrection. There is no reason to doubt that she was among the certain women in the upper room praying in anticipation of the Holy Spirit (Acts 1:14).

Joanna also followed Jesus and supported his ministry through her material, spiritual, and intellectual abilities. She was best known through her marriage to Chuza, Herod's steward (Luke 8:2). The Gospel of Luke indicates that Joanna had economic wealth, political status, and social capital because of her husband's reputation.[12] Her bivocational life as wife and minister in early Palestine is the precursor of contemporary bivocational ministry.

Susanna completes the trio of the women frequently named in the Gospel of Luke. We only know her name and her presence at significant events during the ministry, suffering, death, and resurrection of Jesus. While Scripture does not indicate the identity of her kinfolk or whether she was married, she is named among the women who proclaimed the good news to the marginalized while ministering to the needs of Jesus and her male counterparts, the disciples.

We can only speculate about the relationship among the women who followed Jesus because Scripture does not offer details of their conversations with each other or their reflections about their ministry and work. The moniker, "certain women," that Luke offers, and accounts of their significance to the life and ministry of Jesus, implies aspects of their relationship. Activities of the "certain women" are recorded in Luke 8:1–3, Matthew 27:55–28:10, Mark 15:40–41 and 16:1–13, Luke 24:1–11, John 20:1–18, and Acts 1:14. The women worked together promoting and supporting the ministry of Jesus. Together they engaged in teaching, preaching, pastoring, cooking, cleaning, and traveling because they all believed in Jesus and his ministry. We can imagine they offered a powerful example of female evangelists to women and girls throughout Galilee and all Judea. Mary Magdalene was present at the foot of the cross with Mary the mother of Jesus, Joanna, Susanna, Salome, and two other women named Mary. Their presence together during a time of grief and great pain suggests the sacred relationship

12. Ibid., 91.

among women who mourn the loss of a loved one together. Luke notes that certain women were together with the disciples making up the number of 120 believers praying as they waited on the coming of the Holy Spirit. The deeds of certain women commissions the church to advocate for femaleship among women and girls. The divine nature of their relationships can propel the church and its ministry beyond expectations.

How does the church support and advocate for unique and creative ministries of women and girls?

What is the nature of pastoral care given to women and girls, especially those who are black/white mixed-race? What is the unique way that women and girls mourn and grieve, and how does the church support them in this?

How does the church enhance love, joy, peace, patience, and other fruits of the spirit for women and girls?

How does the church facilitate women and girls' femaleship, both within the church and in public spaces?

The Spirit Gives Power to the Church to Show Fortitude

Fortitude is the spiritual and intellectual strength to persevere in spite of overwhelming obstacles of injustice. Fortitude looks impossibility in the face while pressing toward possibility. Women and girls with fortitude are courageous, persistent, and unrelenting for the flourishing of all. The certain women discussed above demonstrated fortitude through their service as disciples of Jesus Christ. His leadership in partnership with the women in his ministry show fortitude for love and justice for all who would believe that Jesus came to bring them abundant life.

Mary Magdalene practiced fortitude as well as femaleship as discussed above. When many believed she would never overcome her illnesses, she met Jesus and was healed. She had the strength and stamina to persist against stereotypes imposed on her personhood. Her determination moved her from the reality of her circumstances as a person scorned because of her illnesses and the mystery of her origins to a resourceful and righteous evangelist in the ministry of Jesus Christ. Mary Magdalene pressed forward to become a noted female disciple—a leader among women and men—who followed Jesus.

Likewise, the nameless "woman who had been suffering from hemorrhages for twelve years" (Mark 5:25) showed fortitude as she sought the healing touch of Jesus. "She had endured much under many physicians, and had spent all that she had; and she was no better, but rather grew worse" (Mark 5:26). She heard about how Jesus had healed others, including women. She braved the large crowd and the laws that forbade menstruating women from being touched. "When a woman has a discharge of blood that is her regular discharge from her body, she shall be in her impurity for seven days, and whoever touches her shall be unclean until the evening" (Leviticus 15:19). If the discharge of blood goes beyond the time of her impurity she is in a state of perpetual uncleanness (Leviticus 15:25). For twelve long years she was denied touch by men or women unless they were prepared to be quarantined for seven days because of the purity laws. Perhaps only menstruating women visited her, sharing conversations and meals as an act of femaleness before they underwent the cleansing ritual. Everything she touched—bed linens, furniture, dishes, clothes— was considered ritually unclean. For twelve years she never had seven days after bleeding had stopped to take two turtledoves or two pigeons to the priest. If she had the pleasure of the seven days of cleanliness of her discharge, on the eighth day she would have taken one bird for a burnt offering and the other for atonement of her sin (Lev 15:28–30).

Despite her perpetual state of uncleanness and isolation, she pressed forward through the massive crowd believing that "If I but touch his clothes, I will be made well" (Mark 5:28). With strength of mind and will she emerged from isolation and despair into the massive crowd, who wanted to be in the presence of Jesus. Timing and position meant everything if she were to be healed. Her perseverance proved profitable and she was immediately healed.

Jesus knew what had happened for he felt the healing power flow from his body. After inquiring about the incident with his clueless disciples, the woman, trembling in fear, fell before him to confess why she had been determined to touch him. She had risked being demonized by religious officials and all others who knew her and about her illness. She feared punishment and eternal ostracizing at the hands of those who honored ritual impurity laws more than the health and wellness of a woman. Her faith fueled her fortitude to be healed by Jesus of her disease.

The challenge to the church is to exemplify fortitude like Mary Magdalene and the unnamed hemorrhaging woman. The world is filled with people who need healing physically and spiritually. The church, the bride of Christ, has a capacity unlike any other institution to heal all that seek its touch.

What is the nature of its power when people who are sick are healed even in the shadow of the church? (Acts 5:15).

How can the church be trusted to hear the truth of those who are afraid and ostracized?

How does the church live out its identity and mission as the body of Christ empowered by the indwelling Spirit of God? When will that day come?

When will the church have the strength to love marginalized women and girls, including the black/white mixed-race young women?

The Spirit Gives Power to the Church to be Free

Freedom is a state of mind that governs the desires of the heart and the actions of the body. Freedom is the ontological ideal practiced in the face of existential bondage. As discussed in chapter 4, authentic identity and agency are two aspects of freedom. An individual or community is free to choose her God-given identity regardless of the shackles of economic, social, and political circumstances. A person or community is also free when they have agency to thrive rather than merely survive.

Jesus modeled such freedom. His engagement with and reception of the marginalized, including women and girls, demonstrates a clear understanding of his identity and agency, as discussed in chapter 4. Scripture captures the numerous times he made clear his identity to those who challenged him throughout his lifetime, starting with temptations by the devil while he was fasting in the wilderness up to the events of his capture and crucifixion.

The interchange with Peter about his identity in Matthew 16:13–20 gives insight for understanding the identity and agency of Jesus Christ. When Jesus asked his disciples, "Who do people say that the Son of Man is?" (v. 13b) they respond John the Baptist, Elijah, and Jeremiah, or one of the prophets (v. 14). When Jesus asked, "But who do you say that I am?" (v. 15) Simon Peter responded, "You are the Messiah, the Son of the living God" (v.16). Jesus answered Peter, "Blessed are you, Simon son of Jonah! For flesh and blood has not revealed this to you, but my Father in heaven. And I tell you, you are Peter, and on this rock I will build my church, and the gates of Hades will not prevail against it. I will give you the keys of the kingdom of heaven, and whatever you bind on earth will be bound in heaven, and whatever you loose on earth will be loosed in heaven" (vv. 17–19). Jesus affirms Peter for articulating his identity as the Messiah, which connotes prophet, priest, and king in first-century Palestine.[13] The signification of king is the focus for Matthew that signals "God's chosen agent for inaugurating the eschatological kingdom of God."[14] The response from Jesus indicates that Peter's divine answer comes directly from God the Father and is not something that Peter could have known as a mortal. Jesus' identity is divinely sanctioned as the Christ—the anointed one, in Greek, and Messiah, in Hebrew, indicating the promise of God to save the people of Israel from injustice. Jesus claims his identity and notes that this belief will be the foundation of the church that he will establish. Jesus also indicates the agency he has in shaping a new community—the church—that will usher in the kingdom that addresses the needs and expectations of the

13. Boring, "The Gospel of Matthew," 357.
14. Ibid.

people of Israel. Jesus is the builder of the church and Peter, the rock, is the foundation upon which the new community must be built.[15] In Matthew 16:13–20 as in Mark 8:27–30 and Luke 9:18–20, Peter declares the identity of Jesus as Messiah and Jesus affirms the divine affirmation of his identity. These passages also indicate the agency Jesus has as Messiah to declare the nature of his lordship, to build a new community, the church, which will prevail eternally.

The identity and agency of Jesus Christ, the Messiah, offers a challenge to the contemporary church to claim its identity and agency.

How is the Christian church authentically the creation of Jesus Christ? What is the foundation of the church that is impenetrable and unshakable?

What agency must the church of Jesus Christ claim in order to manifest the reign of Christ in the world?

How does the identity and agency of the church reflect the needs of black/white mixed-race young women?

This conclusion challenges Christian congregations to consider its practices if it seeks to offer emancipatory hope. The process of emancipatory hope that involves forgiveness, femaleship, fortitude, and freedom is applicable to the entire congregation as well as to all black/white mixed-race women and girls who seek to transform their tragic relationships with other women and girls into healthy life-giving relationships. The congregation that seeks to offer life-giving ministry to all its members must attend to good ministry for young women and girls. A vision for good ministry ought to attend to the specific needs of these women and girls from diverse racial/ethnic backgrounds. A congregation must be courageous to advocate for the thriving of all members through the power of the Holy Spirit. Then and only then will the church disrupt racialization and usher in a post-racial society.

15. Ibid., 344.

Bibliography

Ailey, Alvin. *Alvin Ailey interview.* ArtHaus Musik, 1986.

Ailey, Alvin, with A. Peter Bailey. *Revelations: The Autobiography of Alvin Ailey.* New York: Birch Lane, 1995.

Bae, Hyunju. "Being and Becoming Church: The Spirit–Filled Genesis." https://www.oikoumene.org/en/resources/documents/assembly/2013-busan/bible-studies/being-and-becoming-church-the-spirit-filled-genesis.

Baker-Fletcher, Karen. *Dancing with God: The Trinity from a Womanist Perspective.* St. Louis: Chalice, 2006.

Barnes, Marian E., and Linda Goss, eds. *Talk That Talk: An Anthology of African American Storytelling.* New York: Touchstone, 1989.

Boerman, Tessa, and Samuel Reiziger. *A Knock Out.* DVD. New York: Women Make Movies, 2004.

Bonilla-Silva, Eduardo. "Abstract Liberalism," defined in *ABAGOND.* http://abagond.wordpress.com/2011/10/31/colour–blind–racism–the–four–frames/, July 28, 2014

Bonilla-Silva, Eduardo, and Victor Ray. "It's Real! Racism, Color Blindness, Obama, and the Urgent Need For Social Movement Politics." In *Crisis, Politics and Critical Sociology,* edited by Graham Cassano and Richard A. Dello Buono, 45–58. Boston: Brill, 2010.

Boring, M. Eugene. "The Gospel of Matthew: Introduction, Commentary, and Reflections." In *The New Interpreter's Bible, Volume VIII: New Testament Articles, Matthew,* edited by Leander E. Keck, et al., 353–61. Nashville: Abingdon, 1995.

Bost, Suzanne. *Mulattas and Mestizas: Representing Mixed Identities in the Americas, 1850–2000.* Athens, GA: University of Georgia Press, 2003.

Bultmann, Rudolf. *Theology of the New Testament.* New York: Charles Scribner's Sons, 1951.

Cannon, Katie Geneva. *Katie's Canon: Womanism and the Soul of the Black Community.* Lexington, KY: Continuum, 1995.

Collins, Patricia Hill. *Black Feminist Thought: Knowledge, Consciousness, and the Politics of Empowerment.* 2nd ed. New York: Routledge, 2000.

Coyle, Catherine T. "Forgiveness, Reconciliation, and Healing." In *Forgiveness and Abuse: Jewish and Christian Reflections,* edited by Marie M. Fortune and Joretta Marshall, 98–103. New York: Haworth Pastoral, 2002.

Day, Keri. *Unfinished Business: Black Women, the Black Church, and the Struggle to Thrive in America.* Maryknoll, NY: Orbis, 2012.

Durrow, Heidi W. *The Girl Who Fell from the Sky.* Chapel Hill, NC: Algonquin, 2010.

Fleming, Cynthia G. *Soon We Will Not Cry: The Liberation of Ruby Doris Smith Robinson.* New York: Rowman and Littlefield, 1998.

Giddings, Paula. *When and Where I Enter: The Impact of Black Women on Race and Sex in America.* New York: Bantam, 1984.

Harris, Maria. *Fashion Me A People: Curriculum in the Church.* Louisville: Westminster John Knox, 1989.

Hurston, Zora Neale. *Their Eyes Were Watching God.* New York: Harper and Row, 1937.

John, Esther. "I am Your Sister." *Lesbian News* 37:5 (2011) 22–25.

Joiner, Lottie L. "Visible Lives: African American Artists Use Their Craft to Dispel Myths About the Black Gay Experience." *The Crisis* 1, Winter (2012) 30–34.

Jolivette, Andrew J, ed. *Obama and the Biracial Factor: The Battle for a New American Majority.* Bristol: Policy, 2012.

Jones, Arthur. *Wade in the Water: The Wisdom of the Spirituals.* Boulder, CO: Leave a Little Room, 2005.

Kilson, Marion. *Claiming Place: Biracial Young Adults of the Post-Civil Rights Era.* Westport, CT: Bergin and Garvey, 2001.

King, Martin Luther, Jr. *Strength to Love.* Minneapolis: Fortress, 1963.

Lamis, Dorian A., and David Lester. "Risk Factors for Suicidal Ideation Among African American and European American College Women." *Psychology of Women Quarterly* 36:3 (2012) 337–49.

Marshall, Joretta L. "Communal Dimensions of Forgiveness: Learning From the Life and Death of Matthew Shepard." *Journal of Pastoral Theology* 9 (1999) 49–61.

Marshall, Joretta L. "Forgiving Churches: Avenues of Hope for Rural Communities." *Word and World* 20:1 (2000) 188–92.

Mawhinney, Lynnette. "Othermothering: A Personal Narrative Exploring Relationships between Black Female Faculty and Students." *Negro Educational Review* 62–63:1–4 (2011–2012) 213–32.

McAvoy, Jane. "The Practice of Forgiveness in Sue Miller's Novel *The World Below.*" In *Forgiveness and Abuse: Jewish and Christian Reflections,* edited by Marie M. Fortune and Joretta Marshall, 135–45. New York: Haworth Pastoral, 2002.

McKim, Donald K. *Westminster Dictionary of Theological Terms.* Louisville: Westminster John Knox, 1996.

Morrison, Toni. *The Bluest Eye.* New York: Plume, 1994.

———. *Sula.* New York: Knopf, 1973.

Mosbacher, Dee, and Frances Reid. *All God's Children*. DVD. San Francisco: Woman Vision, 1996.

Murphy, Yvette, et al. *Incorporating Intersectionality in Social Work Practice, Research, Policy, and Education*. Washington, DC: NASW, 2009.

Parker, Evelyn. *Trouble Don't Last Always: Emancipatory Hope Among African American Adolescents*. Cleveland: Pilgrim, 2003.

Raimon, Eve Allegra. *The "Tragic Mulatta" Revisited: Race and Nationalism in Nineteenth-Century Antislavery Fiction*. New Brunswick, NJ: Rutgers University Press, 2004.

Rees, Dee. *I Am Not Broken, I am Free—Pariah*, Spoken by Alike (Adepero Oduye). https://lenettgrahm.wordpress.com/2012/12/27/i-am-not-broken-i-am -free-parish/6/27/2015.

Rockquemore, Kerry Ann, and Tracey Laszloffy. *Raising Biracial Children*. New York: AltaMira, 2005.

Sanchez, Sonia. *Wounded in the House of a Friend*. Boston: Beacon, 1995.

Senna, Danzy. *Caucasia*. New York: Riverhead, 1998.

Sewell, Abigail A. "17th December 2008 Moving Beyond Race: Sizing Up Post-Racial Ideologies." July 23, 2014. http://abigailasewell.blogpost. com/2008/12/moving-beyone-race-sizing-up-post.html.

Sims, Angela D., F. Douglas Powe, and Johnny Bernard Hill. *Religio-Political Narratives in the United States: From Martin Luther King, Jr. to Jeremiah Wright*. London: Palgrave Macmillan, 2014.

Stone, Judith. *When She Was White: The True Story of a Family Divided by Race*. New York: Miramax, 2007.

Thurman, Howard. *Deep is the Hunger: Meditations for Apostles of Sensitiveness*. Richmond, IN: Friends United, 1973.

Townes, Emilie. *Womanist Ethics and the Cultural Production of Evil*. New York: Palgrave, 2006.

Walker, Alice. *The Color Purple*. Boston: Harcourt Brace Jovanovich, 1982.

Weems, Renita J. *Just A Sister Away: A Womanist Vision of Women's Relationships in the Bible*. San Diego: LuraMedia, 1988.

Williams, Monica. "Colorblind Ideology is a Form of Racism." *Psychology Today*. December, 2011. http://www.psychologytoday.com/em/83528.

Wise, Tim. *Colorblind: The Rise of Post-Racial Politics and the Retreat from Racial Equity*. San Francisco: City Light, 2010.

Name/Subject Index

Scripture Index

Made in the USA
Middletown, DE
29 November 2017